rib-ticklers

M·A·T·H

Strengthening Basic Skills with Jokes, Comics, and Riddles

GRADE 4

W9-AXN-241

Credits

Author: Darcy Andries

Editor: Barrie Hoople

Cover and Layout Design: Chasity Rice

Inside Illustrations: Christian Elden

Cover Illustration: Rich Powell

This book has been correlated to state, national, and Canadian provincial standards. Visit *www.carsondellosa.com* to search for and view its correlations to your standards.

ISBN 978-1-60418-143-2

01-023121151

Jump Right In

Use >, <, or = to compare each pair of numbers. Circle the letter next to the greater number. If the numbers are equal, circle both letters. To solve the riddle, write the circled letters in order on the answer lines.

1. **S** 626 ◯ 616 **R**

2. **H** 973 ◯ 937 **D**

3. **T** 2,414 ◯ 2,419 **E**

4. **W** 5,874 ◯ 5,784 **C**

5. **A** 3,864 ◯ 3,864 **N**

6. **L** 5,142 ◯ 5,442 **T**

7. **N** 8.02 ◯ 8.12 **E**

8. **D** 9.4 ◯ 9.3 **S**

9. **N** 5.01 ◯ 5.10 **T**

10. **O** 7.5 ◯ 7.50 **T**

11. **R** 0.78 ◯ 0.88 **E**

12. **S** 2.93 ◯ 2.93 **T**

13. **T** 59.9 ◯ 5.99 **P**

14. **I** 9.1 ◯ 9.2 **H**

15. **E** $\frac{1}{2}$ ◯ $\frac{5}{10}$ **W**

16. **A** $\frac{1}{3}$ ◯ $\frac{1}{4}$ **Y**

17. **T** $\frac{1}{4}$ ◯ $\frac{1}{6}$ **A**

18. **K** $\frac{4}{5}$ ◯ $\frac{5}{6}$ **E**

19. **R** $\frac{2}{3}$ ◯ $\frac{1}{3}$ **C**

20. **S** $\frac{1}{2}$ ◯ $\frac{2}{5}$ **T**

Why did the teacher jump into the pool?

Answer:

Because _____ _____ _____   _____   _____

"_____ _____ _____"   _____ _____ _____

Over the Fields

To solve the riddle, connect the dots in order.

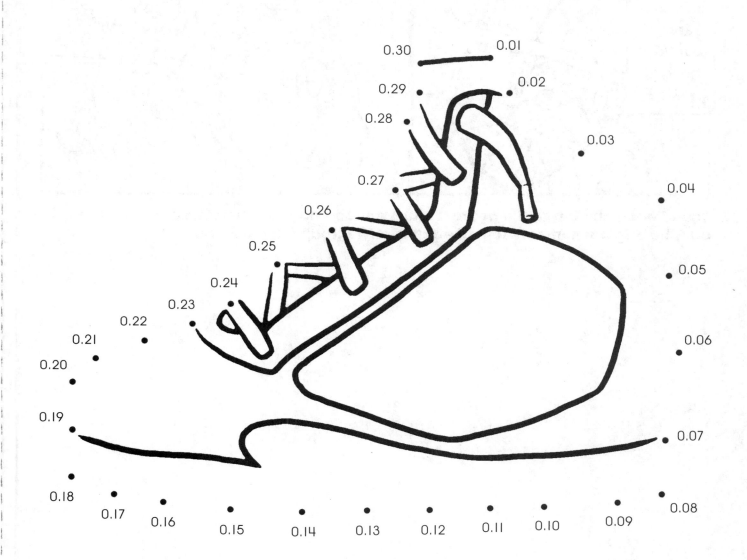

During the day, I walk through streets and run through fields. I might sit under the bed at night, but I am not alone. My tongue hangs out, and I patiently wait to be worn again in the morning.

What am I? _____

Round 'Em Up

Round each number to the nearest thousand and add to estimate each sum. Then, add the original numbers to find each sum. Regroup if necessary.

1.   1,102
     + 6,206

2.   1,508
     + 2,428

3.   1,747
     + 5,844

4.   1,787
     + 3,154

5.   3,736
     + 5,256

6.   3,971
     + 3,385

7.   2,819
     + 5,112

8.   3,090
     + 3,303

9.   7,603
     + 1,968

10.   3,033
     + 4,456

11.   6,873
     + 1,837

12.   2,606
     + 7,025

Jump Around

The numbers below are in expanded form. Write the numbers in standard form. Match each answer with the correct letter in the key. To solve the riddle, write the letters in order on the answer lines.

16,311 = R	26,127 = S	38,525 = O	41,984 = U
51,263 = F	66,418 = G	75,317 = C	87,478 = W
95,175 = P	639,121 = T	713,923 = I	827,677 = H

What is green, jumps, and needs to be scared?

1. $50,000 + 1,000 + 200 + 60 + 3 =$

2. $10,000 + 6,000 + 300 + 10 + 1 =$

3. $30,000 + 8,000 + 500 + 20 + 5 =$

4. $60,000 + 6,000 + 400 + 10 + 8 =$

5. $80,000 + 7,000 + 400 + 70 + 8 =$

6. $700,000 + 10,000 + 3,000 + 900 + 20 + 3 =$

7. $600,000 + 30,000 + 9,000 + 100 + 20 + 1 =$

8. $800,000 + 20,000 + 7,000 + 600 + 70 + 7 =$

9. $(8 \times 100,000) + (2 \times 10,000) + (7 \times 1,000) + (6 \times 100) + (7 \times 10) + (7 \times 1) =$

10. $(7 \times 100,000) + (1 \times 10,000) + (3 \times 1,000) + (9 \times 100) + (2 \times 10) + (3 \times 1) =$

11. $(7 \times 10,000) + (5 \times 1,000) + (3 \times 100) + (1 \times 10) + (7 \times 1) =$

12. 7 ten thousands, 5 thousands, 3 hundreds, 1 ten, and 7 ones =

13. 4 ten thousands, 1 thousand, 9 hundreds, 8 tens, and 4 ones =

14. 9 ten thousands, 5 thousands, 1 hundred, 7 tens, and 5 ones =

15. 2 ten thousands, 6 thousands, 1 hundred, 2 tens, and 7 ones =

Answer: A ___ ___ ___ ___   ___ ___ ___ ___

___ ___ ___ ___ ___ ___ ___ ___

Name: _____

Prime Time

Follow the prime numbers to help Nadia get home.

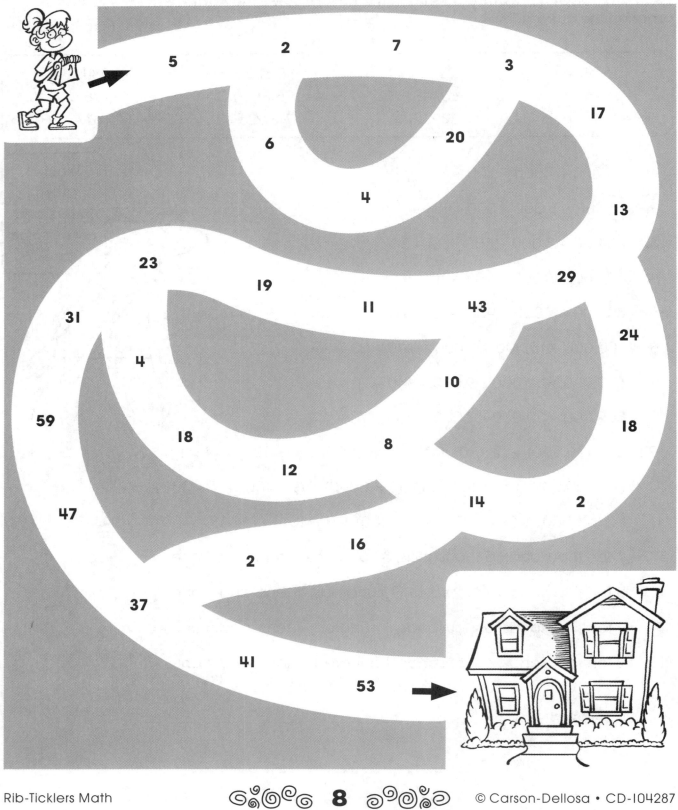

Fresh Breath

Add to find each sum. Regroup if necessary. Match each sum with the correct letter in the key. To solve the riddle, write the letters in order on the answer lines.

93 = D	144 = H	516 = R	889 = B
1,033 = T	6,708 = A	7,182 = E	

1. 116
  + 28

2. 2,570
  + 4,612

3. 52
  + 92

4. 4,321
  + 2,387

5. 12
  + 81

6. 810
  + 79

7. 5,145
  + 1,563

8. 622
  + 411

9. 536
  + 353

10. 486
  + 30

11. 6,358
  + 824

12. 5,057
  + 1,651

13. 875
  + 158

14. 76
  + 68

Why did the bat brush his teeth?

Answer: Because ___ ___   ___ ___ ___   " ___ ___ ___ "

___ ___ ___ ___ ___

Name: _____

Hocus-Pocus

Add to find each sum. Regroup if necessary. To solve the riddle, match the sums to the numbers below and write the correct letters on the answer lines. Hint: Some of the letters will be used more than once.

1. 314
  + 562
  O

2. 874
  + 893
  B

3. 882
  + 999
  N

4. 307
  + 692
  I

5. 686
  + 734
  A

6. 2,527
  + 469
  C

7. 2,815
  + 673
  H

8. 3,238
  + 405
  E

9. 5,123
  + 3,011
  R

10. 5,506
  + 2,002
  T

11. 6,869
  + 2,130
  K

12. 2,376
  + 1,484
  L

13. 2,053
  + 8,761
  Y

14. 4,005
  + 7,090
  U

15. 3,212
  + 3,391
  Q

16. 4,909
  + 2,080
  S

Why do magicians do so well on tests?

Answer: __ __ __ __ __ __ __   __ __ __ __
1,767 3,643 2,996 1,420 11,095 6,989 3,643   7,508 3,488 3,643 10,814

__ __ __ __   " __ __ __ __ __ "
3,860 999 8,999 3,643   7,508 8,134 999 2,996 8,999

__ __ __ __ __ __ __ __ __
6,603 11,095 3,643 6,989 7,508 999 876 1,881 6,989

Sum It Up

Add to find each sum. Regroup if necessary. Then, complete the crossword puzzle.

Across

4. 183,982 + 81,294 =

7. 10,893 + 14,373 =

9. 43,273 + 10,586 =

11. 36,878 + 20,557 =

13. 506,291 + 112,867 =

14. 493,422 + 292,434 =

16. 20,893 + 68,352 =

Down

1. 472,936 + 453,250 =

2. 52,816 + 240,910 =

3. 73,856 + 51,313 =

5. 16,081 + 36,584 =

6. 392,421 + 30,530 =

8. 176,316 + 89,433 =

10. 210,223 + 594,394 =

12. 328,733 + 18,331 =

15. 417,846 + 451,135 =

To the Point

Add to find each sum. Regroup if necessary. Match each sum with the correct letter in the key. To solve the riddle, write the letters in order on the answer lines.

8.21 = O	8.41 = C	9.36 = E	11.20 = I	11.89 = P	12.17 = A
15.66 = N	20.96 = L	22.77 = T	32.29 = D	37.12 = M	

1. 6.35
    + 5.82

2. 12.38
    + 19.91

3. 7.52
    + 1.84

4. 7.61
    + 0.80

5. 5.37
    + 5.83

6. 14.85
    + 22.27

7. 10.30
    + 1.87

8. 17.67
    + 3.29

9. 3.91
    + 7.98

10. 4.58
     + 3.63

11. 8.43
     + 2.77

12. 6.76
     + 8.90

13. 18.97
     + 3.80

What can you put between 2 and 3 to make the result greater than 2, but less than 3?

Answer: ___ ___ ___ ___ ___ ___ ___ ___

___ ___ ___ ___ ___

Playing Games

Subtract to find each difference. Regroup if necessary. To solve the riddle, match the differences to the numbers below and write the correct letters on the answer lines. Hint: Not all of the letters will be used, and some of the letters will be used more than once.

1. $\begin{array}{r} 43 \\ -24 \\ \hline \end{array}$ **O**

2. $\begin{array}{r} 74 \\ -58 \\ \hline \end{array}$ **C**

3. $\begin{array}{r} 72 \\ -52 \\ \hline \end{array}$ **N**

4. $\begin{array}{r} 997 \\ -\ 87 \\ \hline \end{array}$ **H**

5. $\begin{array}{r} 669 \\ -\ 91 \\ \hline \end{array}$ **R**

6. $\begin{array}{r} 352 \\ -\ 75 \\ \hline \end{array}$ **B**

7. $\begin{array}{r} 642 \\ -275 \\ \hline \end{array}$ **T**

8. $\begin{array}{r} 885 \\ -211 \\ \hline \end{array}$ **L**

9. $\begin{array}{r} 822 \\ -143 \\ \hline \end{array}$ **A**

10. $\begin{array}{r} 4{,}243 \\ -\ 270 \\ \hline \end{array}$ **D**

11. $\begin{array}{r} 7{,}629 \\ -\ 799 \\ \hline \end{array}$ **U**

12. $\begin{array}{r} 2{,}585 \\ -\ 124 \\ \hline \end{array}$ **S**

13. $\begin{array}{r} 7{,}580 \\ -2{,}190 \\ \hline \end{array}$ **E**

14. $\begin{array}{r} 7{,}897 \\ -6{,}089 \\ \hline \end{array}$ **M**

15. $\begin{array}{r} 8{,}157 \\ -7{,}351 \\ \hline \end{array}$ **Y**

Why don't zoo animals play games?

Answer: ___ ___ ___ ___ ___ ___ ___   ___ ___ ___ ___ ___
277 5,390 16 679 6,830 2,461 5,390   367 910 5,390 578 5,390

___ ___ ___   ___ ___ ___   ___ ___ ___ ___
679 578 5,390   367 19 19   1,808 679 20 806

" ___ ___ ___ ___ ___   ___ ___ ___ "
16 910 5,390 5,390 367   679 910 2,461

Out of Reach

Subtract to find each difference. Regroup if necessary. Then, complete the crossword puzzle.

Across

2. $2,535 - 2,172 =$

4. $2,440 - 2,334 =$

5. $4,311 - 564 =$

8. $9,379 - 4,312 =$

10. $3,146 - 454 =$

13. $8,446 - 5,156 =$

14. $694 - 157 =$

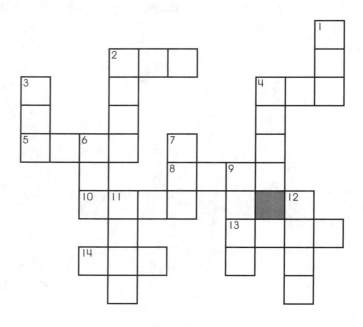

Down

1. $1,230 - 954 =$

2. $6,633 - 3,266 =$

3. $3,267 - 3,114 =$

4. $1,998 - 741 =$

6. $872 - 380 =$

7. $987 - 235 =$

9. $8,546 - 2,009 =$

11. $7,036 - 903 =$

12. $4,036 - 2,072 =$

Surf's Up

Subtract to find each difference. Regroup if necessary. Then, complete the crossword puzzle.

Across

2. 66,859 – 34,437 =

3. 7,495 – 6,816 =

6. 77,528 – 68,431 =

7. 214,965 – 104,426 =

9. 7,689 – 6,726 =

10. 2,276 – 1,562 =

11. 8,173 – 7,289 =

14. 63,207 – 8,009 =

Down

1. 27,791 – 13,782 =

4. 87,223 – 8,224 =

5. 73,461 – 3,861 =

7. 376,912 – 246,506 =

8. 5,510 – 2,102 =

10. 126,827 – 53,320 =

12. 79,998 – 36,948 =

13. 468,446 – 54,863 =

Back to School

Subtract to find each difference. Regroup if necessary. To solve the riddle, match the differences to the numbers below and write the correct letters on the answer lines. Hint: All of the letters will not be used, and some of the letters will be used more than once.

1. 8.26
   − 4.49
      E

2. 93.68
   − 51.44
      H

3. 8.51
   − 0.40
      N

4. 13.69
   − 2.98
      C

5. 71.70
   − 8.19
      O

6. 4.41
   − 2.40
      T

7. 28.50
   − 11.26
      I

8. 49.43
   − 26.52
      A

9. 94.69
   − 21.48
      L

10. 84.24
    − 70.58
       F

11. 8.75
    − 5.50
       R

12. 0.84
    − 0.68
       K

13. 5.94
    − 3.34
       P

14. 83.12
    − 50.74
       D

15. 70.45
    − 69.14
       S

16. 5.55
    − 4.26
       U

What happens to a burger that misses a lot of school?

Answer: __ __ __ __ __ __ __ __ __ __
        17.24 2.01   42.24 22.91 1.31   2.01 63.51   32.38 63.51   22.91

__ __ __ __ __ " __ __ __ __ __ __ __ __ ."
73.21 63.51 2.01   63.51 13.66   0.16 3.77 2.01 10.71 42.24 1.29 2.60

On the Bench

Add or subtract to solve each problem. Regroup if necessary.

1. On Monday, 9,403 people watched the Austin Ants game. On Thursday, 5,474 people watched their game. How many total people watched both games?

2. On Friday, 34,274 fans watched the Montgomery Marsupials play. If the stadium seats 37,928 people, how many seats were empty?

3. The Norfolk Newts traveled 76.6 miles to their first game and 36.2 miles to their second game. How many total miles did the Norfolk Newts travel?

4. The cost of one adult's ticket to a Springfield Sharks game is $26.48. The cost of one child's ticket is $12.59. How much more is one adult's ticket than one child's ticket?

5. On Saturday, 32,875 people watched the Edmonton Eagles and the Columbia Cobras play live, and 226,188 people watched the game on television. How many total people watched the game?

6. On Sunday, 76,847 people watched the Spectacular Series live, and 149,373 people watched it on television. How many more people watched the Spectacular Series on television than watched it live?

Name: _____

Play Me a Tune

Multiply to find each product. To solve the riddle, match the products to the numbers below and write the correct letters on the answer lines. Hint: Some of the letters will be used more than once.

1. 70
    × 3
    B

2. 80
    × 4
    Y

3. 30
    × 3
    K

4. 70
    × 6
    U

5. 40
    × 2
    E

6. 40
    × 9
    T

7. 60
    × 2
    A

8. 70
    × 8
    O

9. 50
    × 6
    C

10. 30
    × 8
    H

11. 60
    × 9
    L

12. 80
    × 6
    I

13. 50
    × 7
    N

14. 30
    × 5
    W

15. 60
    × 3
    P

16. 20
    × 5
    S

Why doesn't the piano work?

Answer: ___ ___ ___ ___ ___ ___ ___   ___ ___
         210 80 300 120 420 100 80   480 360

___ ___ ___ ___   ___ ___ ___ ___ ___   ___ ___ ___
560 350 540 320   90 350 560 150 100   240 560 150

___ ___   " ___ ___ ___ ___ "
360 560   180 540 120 320

Name: _____

Camping Out

Multiply to find each product. To solve the riddle, match the products to the numbers below and write the correct letters on the answer lines. Hint: All of the letters will not be used, and some of the letters will be used more than once.

1. 82
   × 5
   T

2. 97
   × 4
   U

3. 41
   × 6
   L

4. 38
   × 7
   F

5. 66
   × 8
   O

6. 67
   × 9
   H

7. 27
   × 6
   A

8. 34
   × 9
   G

9. 68
   × 7
   N

10. 59
   × 5
   E

11. 24
   × 3
   I

12. 41
   × 4
   S

What did one campfire say to the other?

Answer: ___ ___ ___ , ___ " ___ ___ ___ ___ ___ " ___ ___ ___
     246 295 410 164   306 528   528 388 410   528 476 295

___ ___ ___ ___ ___ ___ ___ ___ ___ ___ ___ ___ .
528 266   410 603 295 164 295   476 72 306 603 410 164

Rib-Ticklers Math   **19**   © Carson-Dellosa • CD-104287

Flower Power

Multiply to find each product. Then, complete the crossword puzzle.

Across

6.   916 × 7 =

7.   232 × 4 =

8.   335 × 5 =

9.   147 × 2 =

10. 639 × 9 =

12. 774 × 6 =

13. 934 × 6 =

15. 127 × 3 =

Down

1.   747 × 6 =

2.   829 × 3 =

3.   847 × 5 =

4.   665 × 9 =

5.   768 × 8 =

11. 142 × 5 =

13. 142 × 4 =

14. 941 × 5 =

Work It Out

Multiply to find each product. To solve the riddle, match the products to the numbers below and write the correct letters on the answer lines. Hint: All of the letters will not be used, and some of the letters will be used more than once.

1.   22
  × 44
G
	2. 43
	  × 23
	C
		3. 30
		  × 30
		A
			4. 34
			  × 12
			E
				5. 21
				  × 31
				M

6.   11
  × 13
D
	7. 80
	  × 11
	T
		8. 51
		  × 15
		I
			9. 41
			  × 21
			P
				10. 21
				  × 33
				J

11.   70
  × 11
N
	12. 11
	  × 45
	O
		13. 30
		  × 31
		R
			14. 33
			  × 12
			L
				15. 14
				  × 16
				U

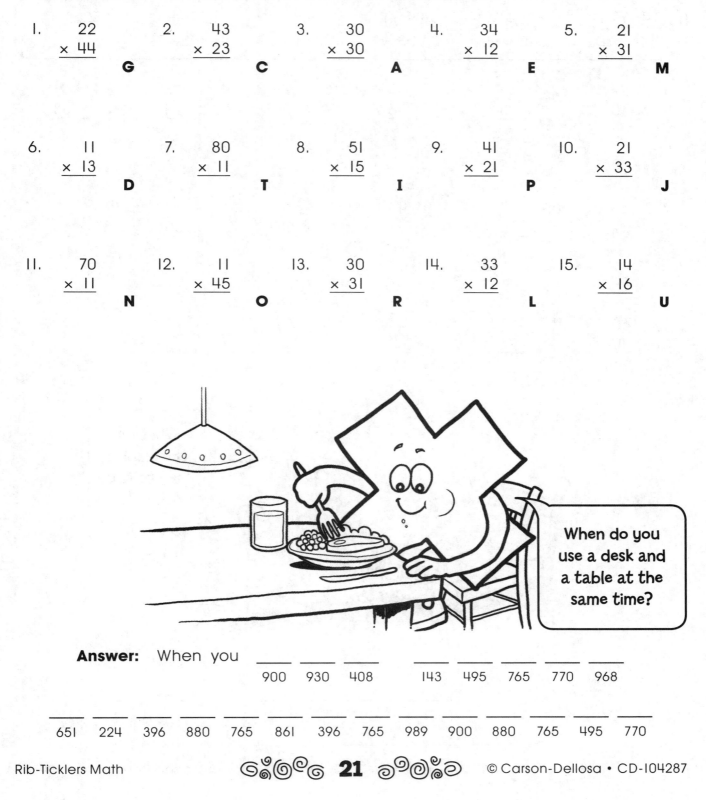

When do you use a desk and a table at the same time?

Answer: When you ___ ___ ___ ___ ___ ___ ___ ___
900 930 408 143 495 765 770 968

___ ___ ___ ___ ___ ___ ___ ___ ___ ___ ___ ___ ___ ___
651 224 396 880 765 861 396 765 989 900 880 765 495 770

Security Blanket

Multiply to find each product. Match each product with the correct letter in the key. To solve the riddle, write the letters in order on the answer lines.

486 = I	825 = V	999 = R	1,105 = Y	1,296 = U	1,520 = O
2,112 = D	2,400 = E	3,003 = T	3,604 = C	6,305 = G	

1. 27
    × 18

2. 33
    × 25

3. 30
    × 80

4. 65
    × 97

5. 76
    × 20

6. 91
    × 33

7. 65
    × 17

8. 40
    × 38

9. 48
    × 27

10. 68
    × 53

11. 19
    × 80

12. 55
    × 15

13. 60
    × 40

14. 37
    × 27

15. 48
    × 50

16. 66
    × 32

What did the blanket say to the bed?

Answer: ____ ' ____ ____   ____ ____ ____   ____ ____ ____

"____ ____ ____ ____ ____ ____ ____."

22

Name: _____

Snow Day

Multiply to find each product. Then, complete the crossword puzzle.

Across

3. 314 × 26 =

6. 58 × 61 =

7. 851 x 85 =

9. 544 × 39 =

12. 41 × 43 =

13. 332 × 25 =

14. 527 × 42 =

15. 53 × 77 =

Down

1. 98 × 86 =

2. 94 × 48 =

4. 281 × 49 =

5. 121 × 37 =

8. 117 × 45 =

10. 335 × 44 =

11. 752 × 41 =

13. 917 × 94 =

Just a Second . . .

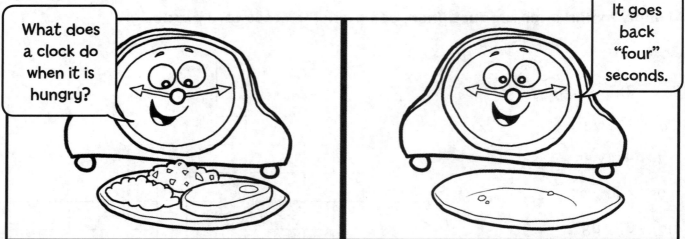

Multiply to find each product.

1. Rupert baked 5 apple pies for a bake sale. If each pie used 12 apples, how many total apples did Rupert use?

2. Tyler made 6 batches of biscuits. He made 24 biscuits in each batch. How many total biscuits did Tyler make?

3. During lunch, students eat 32 bags of pretzel rods. If each bag holds 20 pretzel rods, how many total pretzel rods do students eat?

4. Lisa made 18 blueberry muffins. If each muffin used 13 blueberries, how many total blueberries did Lisa use?

5. Brenda served 25 dishes of fruit. If each dish of fruit had 17 pieces of fruit, how many total pieces of fruit did Brenda serve?

6. Perry sold 24 boxes of crackers. If each box holds 32 crackers, how many total crackers did Perry sell?

A Different Tune

Divide to find each quotient. Match each quotient with the correct letter in the key. To solve the riddle, write the letters in order on the answer lines.

1 = W	2 = D	3 = G	4 = F	5 = O	6 = H
7 = T	8 = R	9 = Y	10 = E	12 = S	

1. $21 \div 3 =$

2. $18 \div 3 =$

3. $40 \div 4 =$

4. $45 \div 5 =$

5. $24 \div 6 =$

6. $50 \div 10 =$

7. $72 \div 9 =$

8. $36 \div 12 =$

9. $45 \div 9 =$

10. $56 \div 8 =$

11. $77 \div 11 =$

12. $54 \div 9 =$

13. $70 \div 7 =$

14. $11 \div 11 =$

15. $10 \div 2 =$

16. $64 \div 8 =$

17. $16 \div 8 =$

18. $144 \div 12 =$

Why do bees hum?

Answer: Because ___ ___ ___ ___ ___   ___ ___ ___ ___ ___ ___ ___

___ ___ ___ ___   ___ ___ ___ ___ ___

Fresh Treats

Divide to find each quotient. Match each remainder with the correct letter in the key. To solve the riddle, write the letters in order on the answer lines.

| 1 = Y | 2 = K | 3 = E | 4 = H | 5 = R | 6 = T | 7 = A | 8 = B |

1. $8\overline{)47}$ 2. $9\overline{)33}$ 3. $7\overline{)55}$ 4. $6\overline{)34}$

5. $4\overline{)31}$ 6. $9\overline{)89}$ 7. $8\overline{)63}$ 8. $7\overline{)47}$

9. $6\overline{)14}$ 10. $6\overline{)51}$ 11. $8\overline{)77}$ 12. $7\overline{)15}$

Where can you buy fresh dog biscuits?

DOG BISCUITS 4 SALE

Answer: ___ ___ ___ " ___ ___ ___ ___ ___ ___ ___ ___ ___ ___ "

Sticky Notes

Divide to find each quotient. To solve the riddle, match the quotients to the numbers below and write the correct letters on the answer lines. Hint: All of the letters will not be used, and some of the letters will be used more than once.

1. 9)837̄ **E**   2. 3)147̄ **I**   3. 2)184̄ **A**   4. 4)868̄ **N**

5. 6)342̄ **O**   6. 5)1,505̄ **P**   7. 8)3,744̄ **L**   8. 2)1,176̄ **S**

9. 5)3,175̄ **D**   10. 4)3,672̄ **Y**

Where do frogs write notes?

Answer: ____ ____   ____ ____ ____ ____   " ____ ____ ____ ____ "
57   217   468   49   468   918   301   92   635   588

Fun in the Sun

Divide to find each quotient. Match each remainder with the correct letter in the key. To solve the riddle, write the letters in order on the answer lines.

1 = E	2 = S	4 = O	5 = R	6 = A	7 = L	8 = B

1. 8)286

2. 4)370

3. 5)224

4. 9)394

5. 7)244

6. 7)180

7. 9)125

8. 2)117

9. 8)262

10. 6)359

What kind of bear likes the sunshine?

Answer: ___ " ___ ___ ___ ___ " ___ ___ ___ ___

Splitting Hairs

Divide to find each quotient. Match each quotient with the correct letter in the key. To solve the riddle, write the letters in order on the answer lines.

19 = E	24 = B	37 = G	43 = A	55 = L	82 = D

1. $22\overline{)946}$ 2. $37\overline{)888}$ 3. $21\overline{)903}$ 4. $15\overline{)825}$ 5. $99\overline{)8,118}$

6. $64\overline{)1,216}$ 7. $61\overline{)2,623}$ 8. $49\overline{)1,813}$ 9. $34\overline{)1,870}$ 10. $85\overline{)1,615}$

Which animal never needs a haircut?

Answer: ____ " ____ ____ ____ ____ " ____ ____ ____ ____

"Dino-mite" Division

Divide to find each quotient. Match each remainder with the correct letter in the key. To solve the riddle, write the letters in order on the answer lines.

2 = H	3 = N	4 = R	5 = O	6 = D	7 = I	8 = S	9 = E

1. $26\overline{)80}$

2. $18\overline{)81}$

3. $14\overline{)76}$

4. $15\overline{)142}$

5. $79\overline{)477}$

6. $56\overline{)453}$

7. $85\overline{)348}$

8. $54\overline{)111}$

9. $36\overline{)329}$

10. $21\overline{)151}$

11. $51\overline{)315}$

12. $28\overline{)232}$

What does an apatosaurus do when he sleeps?

Answer: ____ ____ " ____ ____ ____ - ____ ____ ____ ____ ____ ."

At the Movies

Divide to find each quotient.

1. Alisha bought 21 movie tickets. She divided the tickets evenly between her 7 cousins. How many tickets did each cousin get?

2. Keith divided 84 of his DVDs evenly between 7 of his friends. How many DVDs did each friend get?

3. Samantha divided 48 movies evenly among 8 of her friends. How many movies did each friend get?

4. There were 135 people at the movie theater. If the people split into 9 even groups to watch different movies, how many people watched each movie?

5. There were 352 people at the movie theater. If the people split into 16 even groups to watch different movies, how many people watched each movie?

6. The movie theater donated 648 tickets to 18 schools. If the movie theater donated the same number of tickets to each school, how many tickets did each school receive?

Take Your Best Shot

Determine the divisibility of each number in the table below. To find a quote by Wayne Gretzky, a Hall of Fame hockey player, use the following steps.

1. If the number down is divisible by the number across, circle the letter.
2. If the number down is not divisible by the number across, cross out the letter.
3. Write the circled letters in order from left to right on the answer lines.

ACROSS

	2	3	4	5	6	9
24	Y	O	U	N	M	R
84	I	S	S	L	O	P
18	N	E	V	B	H	U
90	N	D	C	R	E	D
45	L	P	W	E	C	R
96	C	E	N	I	T	X
40	O	S	F	T	R	K
36	H	E	S	Z	H	O
27	R	T	M	L	F	S
42	Y	O	J	M	U	C
20	D	W	O	N	E	G
54	O	T	B	Z	T	A
88	K	Q	E	V	S	N

D O W N

Answer: "___ ___ ___   ___ ___ ___   ___ ___ ___

___ ___   ___ ___ ___ ___ ___ ___

___ ___   ___ ___ ___ ___   ___ ___ ___ ___ ___

___ ___   ___ ___ ___   ___ ___ ___ ___ ___."   – **Wayne Gretzky**

Learning Tree

What kind of math do trees learn?

"Twig-onometry!"

Create a factor tree for each number. The first problem has been done for you.

1. 6
   / \
  3   2

2. 9

3. 21

4. 20

5. 15

6. 12

7. 16

8. 18

9. 24

Name: _____

Roll with Me

Find the least common multiple for each pair of numbers. Match each answer with the correct letter in the key. To solve the riddle, write the letters in order on the answer lines.

8 = O	9 = M	12 = D	15 = R	16 = A	18 = N
20 = H	24 = S	25 = I	27 = C	28 = T	30 = E

1. 25   5

    LCM = ____

2. 7   4

    LCM = ____

3. 4   10

    LCM = ____

4. 16   8

    LCM = ____

5. 4   3

    LCM = ____

6. 3   9

    LCM = ____

7. 8   4

    LCM = ____

8. 3   15

    LCM = ____

9. 10   6

    LCM = ____

10. 9   27

    LCM = ____

11. 6   15

    LCM = ____

12. 9   2

    LCM = ____

13. 4   14

    LCM = ____

14. 12   8

    LCM = ____

Why didn't the quarter roll into the street with the nickel?

Answer: Because ____ ____   ____ ____ ____

____ ____ " ____ ____ ____ ____ "

Sticky Situation

Find the greatest common factor for each pair of numbers. Match each answer with the correct letter in the key. To solve the riddle, write the letters in order on the answer lines.

2 = S	3 = C	4 = U	5 = K	6 = Y
7 = T	9 = I	11 = M	12 = O	15 = N

1. 9   27   2. 33   22   3. 6   10   4. 7   21

   GCF = ____   GCF = ____   GCF = ____   GCF = ____

5. 20   8   6. 12   21   7. 10   35   8. 24   12

   GCF = ____   GCF = ____   GCF = ____   GCF = ____

9. 30   15   10. 36   6   11. 24   36   12. 12   32

   GCF = ____   GCF = ____   GCF = ____   GCF = ____

What did the gum say to the shoe?

Answer: ____ ' ____   " ____ ____ ____ ____ ____ " ____ ____   ____ ____ ____.

Funny Fractions

Write the missing number that makes each pair of fractions equivalent.

1. $\dfrac{1}{5} = \dfrac{}{10}$

2. $\dfrac{1}{2} = \dfrac{2}{}$

3. $\dfrac{1}{3} = \dfrac{9}{}$

4. $\dfrac{1}{6} = \dfrac{}{18}$

5. $\dfrac{4}{5} = \dfrac{8}{}$

6. $\dfrac{1}{3} = \dfrac{3}{}$

7. $\dfrac{1}{5} = \dfrac{}{20}$

8. $\dfrac{3}{5} = \dfrac{15}{}$

9. $\dfrac{}{9} = \dfrac{4}{18}$

10. $\dfrac{}{4} = \dfrac{4}{16}$

11. $\dfrac{}{5} = \dfrac{3}{15}$

12. $\dfrac{1}{2} = \dfrac{}{18}$

13. $\dfrac{}{9} = \dfrac{6}{18}$

14. $\dfrac{1}{} = \dfrac{5}{25}$

15. $\dfrac{2}{} = \dfrac{4}{10}$

16. $\dfrac{}{5} = \dfrac{12}{15}$

17. $\dfrac{3}{} = \dfrac{12}{24}$

18. $\dfrac{4}{} = \dfrac{16}{24}$

Software Upgrade

Reduce each fraction to simplest form. Match each answer with the correct letter in the key. To solve the riddle, write the letters in order on the answer lines.

$\frac{1}{10}$ = I	$\frac{1}{6}$ = G	$\frac{1}{5}$ = E	$\frac{1}{4}$ = M	$\frac{2}{7}$ = O	$\frac{1}{3}$ = T	$\frac{2}{5}$ = S
$\frac{1}{2}$ = B	$\frac{3}{5}$ = R	$\frac{2}{3}$ = W	$\frac{3}{4}$ = H	$\frac{4}{5}$ = V	$\frac{5}{6}$ = P	

1. $\frac{4}{12}$ = ___ 2. $\frac{4}{14}$ = ___ 3. $\frac{3}{30}$ = ___

4. $\frac{4}{16}$ = ___ 5. $\frac{25}{30}$ = ___ 6. $\frac{9}{15}$ = ___

7. $\frac{10}{35}$ = ___ 8. $\frac{8}{10}$ = ___ 9. $\frac{2}{10}$ = ___

10. $\frac{5}{50}$ = ___ 11. $\frac{3}{9}$ = ___ 12. $\frac{6}{15}$ = ___

13. $\frac{10}{15}$ = ___ 14. $\frac{4}{20}$ = ___

15. $\frac{3}{6}$ = ___ 16. $\frac{4}{10}$ = ___

Why did the computer buy glasses?

17. $\frac{4}{40}$ = ___ 18. $\frac{3}{18}$ = ___

19. $\frac{6}{8}$ = ___ 20. $\frac{5}{15}$ = ___

Answer: ___ ___ ___ ___ ___ ___ ___ ___ ___

" ___ ___ ___ ___ ___ ___ ___ ___ "

"T" for Two

Draw a line to match each mixed number to the equivalent improper fraction. To solve the riddles, write the letters in order on the answer lines.

1. $4\frac{7}{8}$ $\frac{17}{8}$ O

2. $1\frac{1}{2}$ $\frac{7}{2}$ L

3. $2\frac{1}{8}$ $\frac{39}{7}$ E

4. $3\frac{2}{3}$ $\frac{3}{2}$ T

5. $5\frac{4}{7}$ $\frac{39}{8}$ A

6. $3\frac{1}{2}$ $\frac{11}{3}$ W

Answer: ___ ___ ___ ___ ___ ___

What gets wetter the more it dries?

7. $3\frac{1}{3}$ $\frac{19}{4}$ A

8. $2\frac{5}{9}$ $\frac{23}{5}$ P

9. $3\frac{3}{4}$ $\frac{4}{3}$ T

10. $4\frac{3}{4}$ $\frac{17}{7}$ O

11. $4\frac{3}{5}$ $\frac{10}{3}$ A

12. $2\frac{3}{7}$ $\frac{15}{4}$ E

13. $1\frac{1}{3}$ $\frac{23}{9}$ T

What starts with a t, ends with a t, and is filled with "t"?

Answer: ___ ___ ___ ___ ___ ___ ___

Name: _____

Riddle Time

Order each set of fractions from least to greatest. To solve the riddles, write the letters in order on the answer lines.

What can you wear any time that never goes out of style?

1.

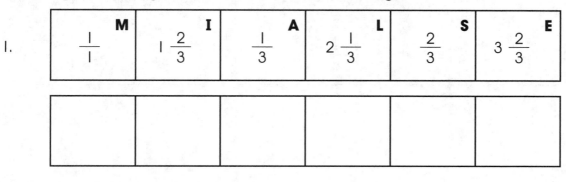

Answer: ____ ____ ____ ____ ____ ____

What goes up but never goes down?

2.

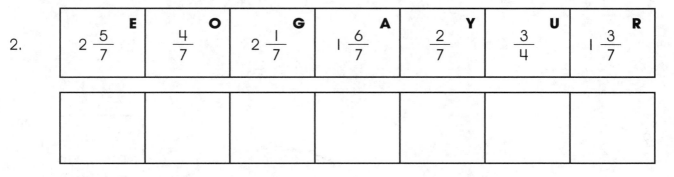

Answer: ____ ____ ____ ____ ____ ____ ____

What go up and down but do not move?

3.

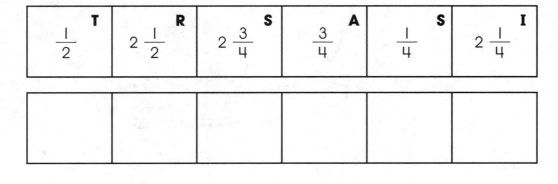

Answer: ____ ____ ____ ____ ____ ____

Just a Phase

Add to find each sum. Match each sum with the correct letter in the key. To solve the riddle, write the letters in order on the answer lines.

$\frac{3}{10}$ = N $\qquad$ $\frac{4}{7}$ = I $\qquad$ $\frac{3}{5}$ = S $\qquad$ $\frac{2}{3}$ = U $\qquad$ $\frac{4}{5}$ = E

$\frac{5}{6}$ = H $\qquad$ $\frac{6}{7}$ = L $\qquad$ $\frac{7}{8}$ = W $\qquad$ $\frac{9}{10}$ = T $\qquad$ $\frac{11}{12}$ = F

1. $\frac{6}{8} + \frac{1}{8} =$ $\qquad\qquad$ 2. $\frac{1}{6} + \frac{4}{6} =$

3. $\frac{2}{5} + \frac{2}{5} =$ $\qquad\qquad$ 4. $\frac{2}{10} + \frac{1}{10} =$

5. $\frac{1}{7} + \frac{3}{7} =$ $\qquad\qquad$ 6. $\frac{7}{10} + \frac{2}{10} =$

7. $\frac{2}{7} + \frac{2}{7} =$ $\qquad\qquad$ 8. $\frac{1}{5} + \frac{2}{5} =$

9. $\frac{7}{12} + \frac{4}{12} =$

10. $\frac{1}{3} + \frac{1}{3} =$

11. $\frac{2}{7} + \frac{4}{7} =$

12. $\frac{5}{7} + \frac{1}{7} =$

When is the moon heaviest?

Answer: ___ ___ ___ ___ ___ ___ ___ ___ " ___ ___ ___ ___ "

Hard Work

Add to find each sum. Reduce each sum to simplest form. Match each sum with the correct letter in the key. To solve the riddle, write the letters in order on the answer lines.

$\frac{1}{7}$ = N $\frac{1}{5}$ = U $\frac{1}{4}$ = O $\frac{1}{3}$ = A $\frac{2}{5}$ = B

$\frac{1}{2}$ = C $\frac{3}{5}$ = T $\frac{2}{3}$ = S $\frac{5}{6}$ = R

1. $\frac{1}{9} + \frac{2}{9} =$

2. $\frac{3}{10} + \frac{1}{10} =$

3. $\frac{1}{8} + \frac{1}{8} =$

4. $\frac{1}{15} + \frac{4}{15} =$

5. $\frac{1}{6} + \frac{2}{6} =$

6. $\frac{2}{12} + \frac{1}{12} =$

7. $\frac{1}{14} + \frac{1}{14} =$

8. $\frac{2}{9} + \frac{4}{9} =$

9. $\frac{2}{10} + \frac{4}{10} =$

10. $\frac{3}{12} + \frac{7}{12} =$

11. $\frac{2}{15} + \frac{1}{15} =$

12. $\frac{1}{8} + \frac{3}{8} =$

13. $\frac{7}{20} + \frac{5}{20} =$

14. $\frac{1}{16} + \frac{3}{16} =$

15. $\frac{7}{18} + \frac{8}{18} =$

What do you call a snake that works?

Answer: ____ ____ ____

" ____ ____ ____ ____ ____ ____ ____ ____ ____ "

Boxed In

Subtract to find each difference. To solve the riddle, match the differences to the numbers below and write the correct letters on the answer lines. Hint: All of the letters will not be used, and some of the letters will be used more than once.

1. $\dfrac{6}{15}$ $-\dfrac{4}{15}$ **T**

2. $\dfrac{8}{9}$ $-\dfrac{6}{9}$ **D**

3. $\dfrac{2}{3}$ $-\dfrac{1}{3}$ **O**

4. $\dfrac{3}{5}$ $-\dfrac{2}{5}$ **I**

5. $\dfrac{6}{7}$ $-\dfrac{3}{7}$ **W**

6. $\dfrac{5}{5}$ $-\dfrac{1}{5}$ **P**

7. $\dfrac{8}{12}$ $-\dfrac{3}{12}$ **S**

8. $\dfrac{6}{8}$ $-\dfrac{3}{8}$ **R**

9. $\dfrac{4}{6}$ $-\dfrac{3}{6}$ **F**

10. $\dfrac{5}{10}$ $-\dfrac{4}{10}$ **H**

11. $\dfrac{6}{7}$ $-\dfrac{1}{7}$ **A**

12. $\dfrac{4}{5}$ $-\dfrac{2}{5}$ **E**

What do you call a cardboard belt?

Answer: ___ " ___ ___ ___ ___ ___ " ___ ___

$\dfrac{5}{7}$ $\dfrac{3}{7}$ $\dfrac{5}{7}$ $\dfrac{1}{5}$ $\dfrac{5}{12}$ $\dfrac{2}{15}$ $\dfrac{1}{3}$ $\dfrac{1}{6}$

___ ___ ___ ___ ___

$\dfrac{4}{5}$ $\dfrac{5}{7}$ $\dfrac{4}{5}$ $\dfrac{2}{5}$ $\dfrac{3}{8}$

Marathon Math

Subtract to find each difference. Reduce each difference to simplest form. Match each difference with the correct letter in the key. To solve the riddle, write the letters in order on the answer lines.

$\frac{1}{6}$ = R $\frac{1}{5}$ = D $\frac{1}{4}$ = Y $\frac{1}{3}$ = T $\frac{2}{5}$ = O $\frac{1}{2}$ = E

$\frac{3}{5}$ = A $\frac{5}{8}$ = L $\frac{2}{3}$ = G $\frac{3}{4}$ = S $\frac{4}{5}$ = W

1. $\frac{4}{12} - \frac{2}{12} =$

2. $\frac{6}{8} - \frac{2}{8} =$

3. $\frac{9}{10} - \frac{3}{10} =$

4. $\frac{9}{10} - \frac{7}{10} =$

5. $\frac{3}{8} - \frac{1}{8} =$

6. $\frac{10}{12} - \frac{1}{12} =$

7. $\frac{12}{14} - \frac{5}{14} =$

8. $\frac{3}{6} - \frac{1}{6} =$

9. $\frac{5}{6} - \frac{1}{6} =$

10. $\frac{20}{24} - \frac{5}{24} =$

11. $\frac{8}{15} - \frac{2}{15} =$

12. $\frac{14}{15} - \frac{2}{15} =$

What is said before fireflies start a race?

Answer: ___ ___ ___ ___ ___,   ___ ___ ___,   "___ ___ ___ ___!"

Higher Learning

Write each fraction as a decimal. To solve the riddle, match the answers to the numbers below and write the correct letters on the answer lines. **Hint: Some of the letters will be used more than once.**

1. $\dfrac{4}{5}$ = _____ **S**

2. $\dfrac{9}{10}$ = _____ **N**

3. $\dfrac{5}{10}$ = _____ **E**

4. $\dfrac{2}{5}$ = _____ **I**

5. $\dfrac{38}{50}$ = _____ **O**

6. $\dfrac{1}{5}$ = _____ **U**

7. $\dfrac{3}{4}$ = _____ **W**

8. $\dfrac{1}{20}$ = _____ **D**

9. $\dfrac{3}{10}$ = _____ **B**

10. $\dfrac{17}{25}$ = _____ **T**

11. $\dfrac{1}{4}$ = _____ **A**

12. $\dfrac{2}{100}$ = _____ **H**

13. $\dfrac{2}{20}$ = _____ **R**

14. $\dfrac{3}{5}$ = _____ **C**

15. $\dfrac{28}{50}$ = _____ **G**

Why did the girl study on the airplane?

Answer: ___ ___ ___ ___ ___ ___ ___   ___ ___ ___
0.3 0.5 0.6 0.25 0.2 0.8 0.5   0.8 0.02 0.5

___ ___ ___ ___ ___ ___ ___ " ___ ___ ___ ___ ___ ___ "
0.75 0.25 0.9 0.68 0.5 0.05 0.25   0.02 0.4 0.56 0.02 0.5 0.1

___ ___ ___ ___ ___ ___ ___ ___ ___
0.5 0.05 0.2 0.6 0.25 0.68 0.4 0.76 0.9

Kick Stand

Write each decimal as a fraction. Reduce each fraction to simplest form. To solve the riddle, match the answers to the numbers below and write the correct letters on the answer lines. Hint: Some of the letters will be used more than once.

1. 0.32 = _____ **W**   2. 0.11 = _____ **T**   3. 0.22 = _____ **A**

4. 0.48 = _____ **E**   5. 0.84 = _____ **R**   6. 0.1 = _____ **U**

7. 0.08 = _____ **D**   8. 0.9 = _____ **B**   9. 0.51 = _____ **O**

10. 0.7 = _____ **I**   11. 0.25 = _____ **S**   12. 0.8 = _____ **C**

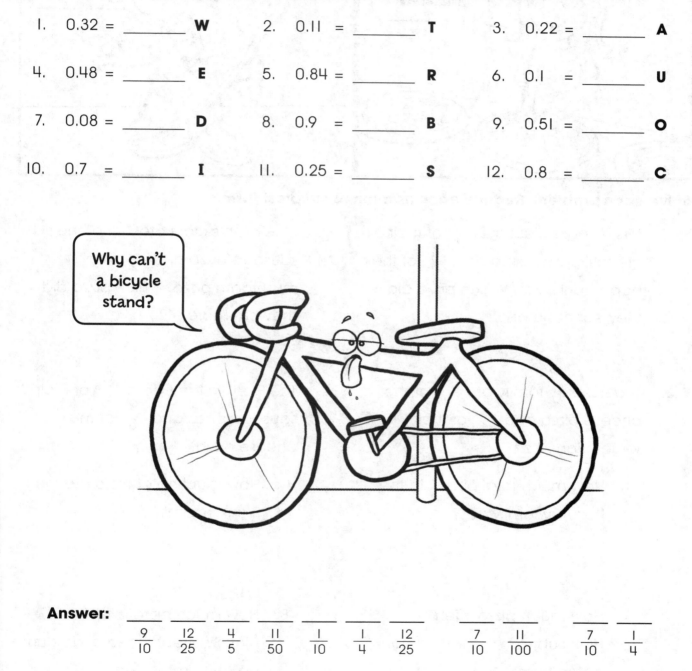

Why can't a bicycle stand?

Answer: ___ ___ ___ ___ ___ ___ ___   ___ ___   ___ ___
$\frac{9}{10}$ $\frac{12}{25}$ $\frac{4}{5}$ $\frac{11}{50}$ $\frac{1}{10}$ $\frac{1}{4}$ $\frac{12}{25}$ $\frac{7}{10}$ $\frac{11}{100}$ $\frac{7}{10}$ $\frac{1}{4}$

"___ ___ ___"   ___ ___ ___ ___ ___
$\frac{11}{100}$ $\frac{8}{25}$ $\frac{51}{100}$ $\frac{11}{100}$ $\frac{7}{10}$ $\frac{21}{25}$ $\frac{12}{25}$ $\frac{2}{25}$

Pizza Slices

Solve each problem. Reduce each fraction to simplest form.

1. Mrs. Avery's class ate $\frac{1}{5}$ of their green pepper pizza and $\frac{2}{5}$ of their pepperoni pizza. Which pizza did they eat more of?

2. Mr. Quinn's class ate $\frac{3}{4}$ of their sausage pizza and $\frac{1}{2}$ of their mushroom pizza. Which pizza did they eat more of?

3. The Roxbury family ate $\frac{1}{3}$ of their cheese pizza and $\frac{2}{3}$ of their vegetarian pizza.

    A. How much total pizza did the Roxbury family eat?

    B. How much pizza is left?
        Hint: Subtract the total amount eaten from $\frac{6}{3}$.

4. The Franklin family ate $\frac{5}{6}$ of their sausage pizza and $\frac{2}{3}$ of their cheese pizza.

    A. How much total pizza did the Franklin family eat?

    B. How much pizza is left?
        Hint: Subtract the total amount eaten from $\frac{12}{6}$.

Measuring Words

What word in the dictionary is the longest?

Smiles, because there is a mile between each *s*.

Use the information below to convert each measurement.

12 inches = 1 foot	5,280 feet = 1 mile
3 feet = 1 yard	1,760 yards = 1 mile

1. _____ inches = 2 feet

2. _____ feet = 2 yards

3. _____ inches = 2 yards

4. 48 inches = _____ feet

5. _____ yards = 3 miles

6. _____ feet = 2 miles

7. _____ inches = 1 mile

8. 12 feet = _____ yards

9. _____ inches = 4 yards

10. 36 inches = _____ feet

11. 7,040 yards = _____ miles

12. _____ feet = 5 miles

13. 108 inches = _____ yards

14. _____ feet = 5 yards

15. _____ inches = 1 yard

16. 15,840 feet = _____ miles

17. 120 inches = _____ feet

18. 3,520 yards = _____ miles

19. _____ inches = 5 yards

20. _____ inches = 5 feet

Rising Flowers

Use the information below to convert each measurement. Match each answer with the correct letter in the key. To solve the riddle, write the letters in order on the answer lines.

8 fluid ounces = 1 cup	2 pints = 1 quart
2 cups = 1 pint	4 quarts = 1 gallon

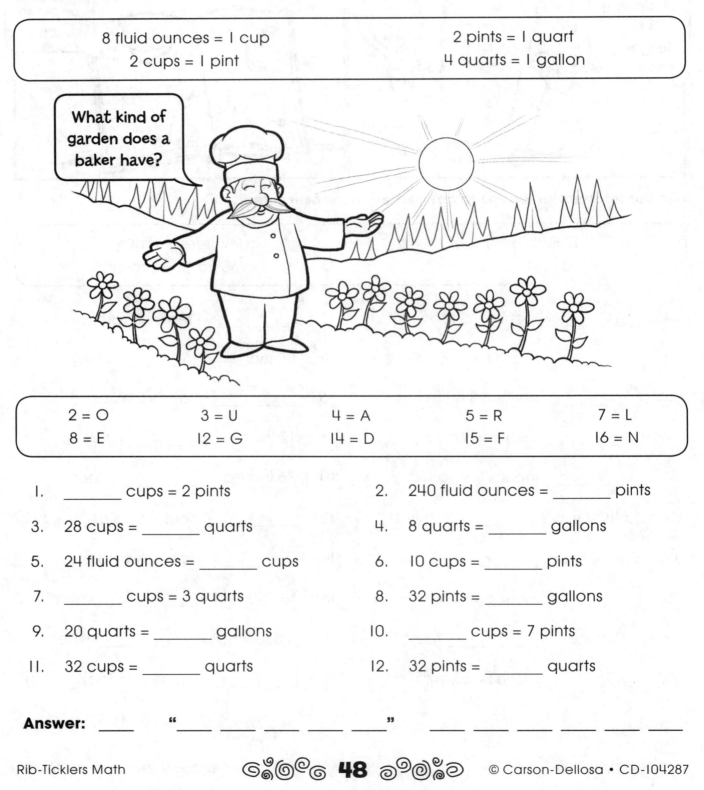

What kind of garden does a baker have?

2 = O	3 = U	4 = A	5 = R	7 = L
8 = E	12 = G	14 = D	15 = F	16 = N

1. _____ cups = 2 pints

2. 240 fluid ounces = _____ pints

3. 28 cups = _____ quarts

4. 8 quarts = _____ gallons

5. 24 fluid ounces = _____ cups

6. 10 cups = _____ pints

7. _____ cups = 3 quarts

8. 32 pints = _____ gallons

9. 20 quarts = _____ gallons

10. _____ cups = 7 pints

11. 32 cups = _____ quarts

12. 32 pints = _____ quarts

Answer: _____ " ___ ___ ___ ___ " ___ ___ ___ ___ ___ ___

The Weight of It All

Use the information below to convert each measurement.

16 ounces = 1 pound	2,000 pounds = 1 ton

1. 160 ounces = _____ pounds

2. _____ ounces = 5 pounds

3. 5 tons = _____ ounces

4. _____ ounces = 9 pounds

5. 4,000 pounds = _____ tons

6. _____ pounds = 7 tons

7. 8,000 pounds = _____ tons

8. _____ ounces = 11 pounds

9. _____ pounds = 3 tons

10. 10 tons = _____ ounces

11. 32 ounces = _____ pounds

12. _____ ounces = 3 pounds

13. 96 ounces = _____ pounds

14. _____ ounces = 7 pounds

15. 128 ounces = _____ pounds

16. _____ tons = 192,000 ounces

17. 192 ounces = _____ pounds

18. _____ ounces = 40 pounds

19. 1 ton = _____ ounces

20. _____ tons = 64,000 ounces

Name: _____

"Liter" of the Pack

Why did the soda bottle take music lessons?

It wanted to be a "band-liter."

Use the information below to convert each measurement.

1 liter (L) = 100 centiliters (cL) = 1,000 milliliters (mL)
1 gram (g) = 100 centigrams (cg) = 1,000 milligrams (mg)
1 meter (m) = 100 centimeters (cm) = 1,000 millimeters (mm)
1 kiloliter (kL) = 1,000 liters (L)
1 kilogram (kg) = 1,000 grams (g)
1 kilometer (km) = 1,000 meters (m)

1. _____ mL = 2 L

2. 25 kg = _____ g

3. 19,000 mL = _____ L

4. _____ L = 3,200 cL

5. _____ m = 400 cm

6. _____ km = 19,000 m

7. _____ cm = 110 mm

8. 8,000 mg = _____ g

9. 6 km = _____ m

10. 4 cg = _____ mg

11. _____ mm = 36 m

12. 7 cL = _____ mL

13. _____ kL = 4,000 L

14. 5,000 mm = _____ m

15. _____ cg = 410 mg

16. 52 m = _____ cm

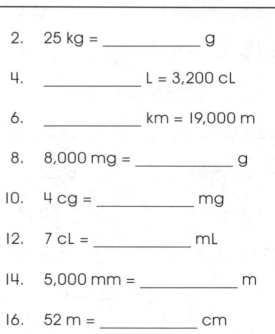

Good Grades

Order each set of measurements from least to greatest.

1. 30 minutes   70 minutes   1 hour   15 minutes   2 hours

    _____

2. 25 hours   2 days   36 hours   1 day   12 hours

    _____

3. 1 gallon   9 pints   5 cups   5 quarts   15 cups

    _____

4. 3 cups   1 pint   1 quart   3 pints   2 quarts

    _____

5. 4 pints   1 quart   3 gallons   6 pints   4 quarts

    _____

6. 1,800 yards   1 foot   1 yard   30 inches   1 mile

    _____

7. 4 feet   4 yards   44 inches   14 inches   4 inches

    _____

8. 33 mm   3 cm   3 m   3 km   33 cm

    _____

Skating Lines

Identify each figure as a point, ray, line, or line segment.

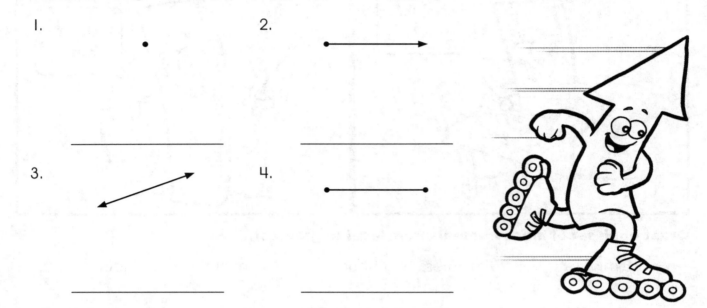

1.

2.

_____

3.

4.

_____

Use letters to name each figure.

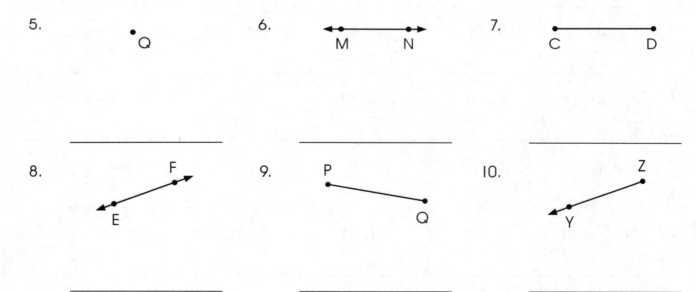

5. Q

6. M N

7. C D

_____

8. F E

9. P Q

10. Z Y

_____

52

Snack Break

Identify each pair of lines as parallel, intersecting, or perpendicular. To solve the riddle, circle the letter indicated in each answer and write the letters in order on the answer lines. The first problem has been done for you.

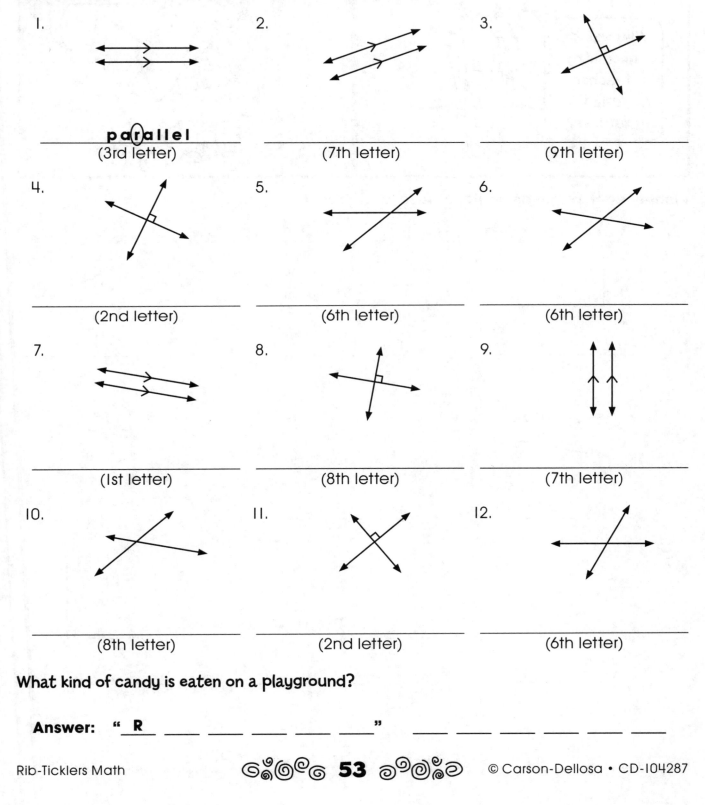

1.

_____
pa(r)allel
(3rd letter)

2.

_____
(7th letter)

3.

_____
(9th letter)

4.

_____
(2nd letter)

5.

_____
(6th letter)

6.

_____
(6th letter)

7.

_____
(1st letter)

8.

_____
(8th letter)

9.

_____
(7th letter)

10.

_____
(8th letter)

11.

_____
(2nd letter)

12.

_____
(6th letter)

What kind of candy is eaten on a playground?

Answer: " **R** ___ ___ ___ ___ ___ " ___ ___ ___ ___ ___ ___

On Crutches

Identify each angle as acute, obtuse, or right.

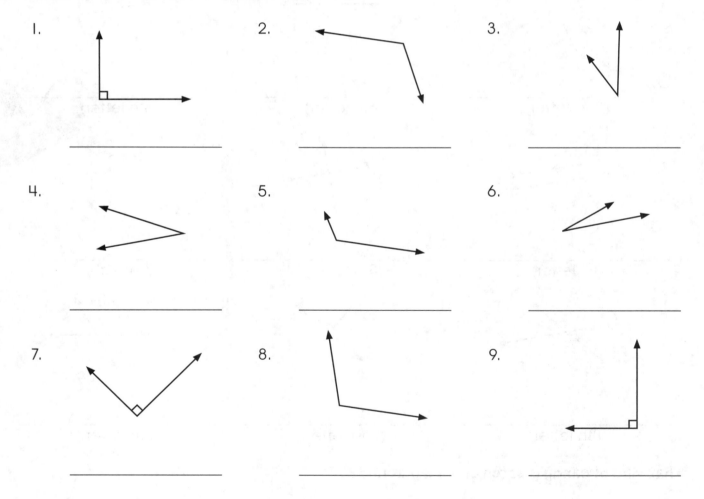

1. _____

2. _____

3. _____

4. _____

5. _____

6. _____

7. _____

8. _____

9. _____

Hidden Shapes

**Identify each triangle. If the triangle appears to be a right triangle, color it green.
If the triangle is an obtuse triangle, color it blue. If the triangle is an acute triangle,
color it purple.**

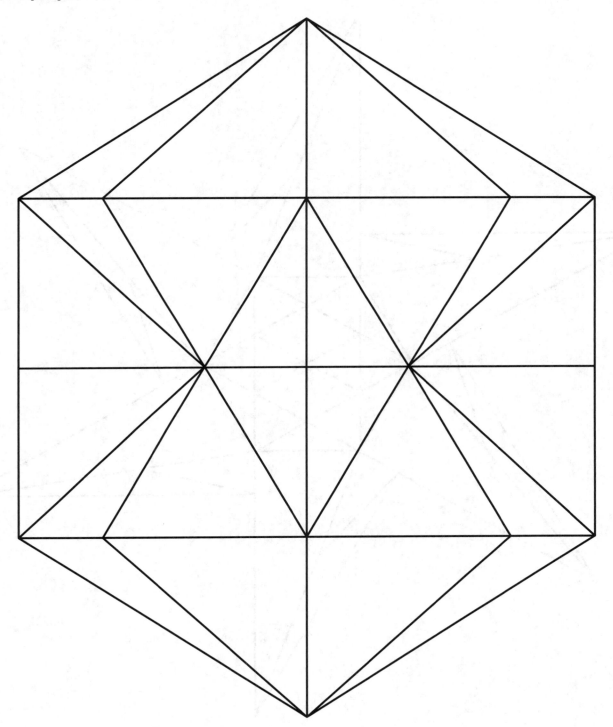

Finding Triangles

Identify each triangle. If the triangle is an isosceles triangle, color it orange. If the triangle is an equilateral triangle, color it red. If the triangle is a scalene triangle, color it yellow.

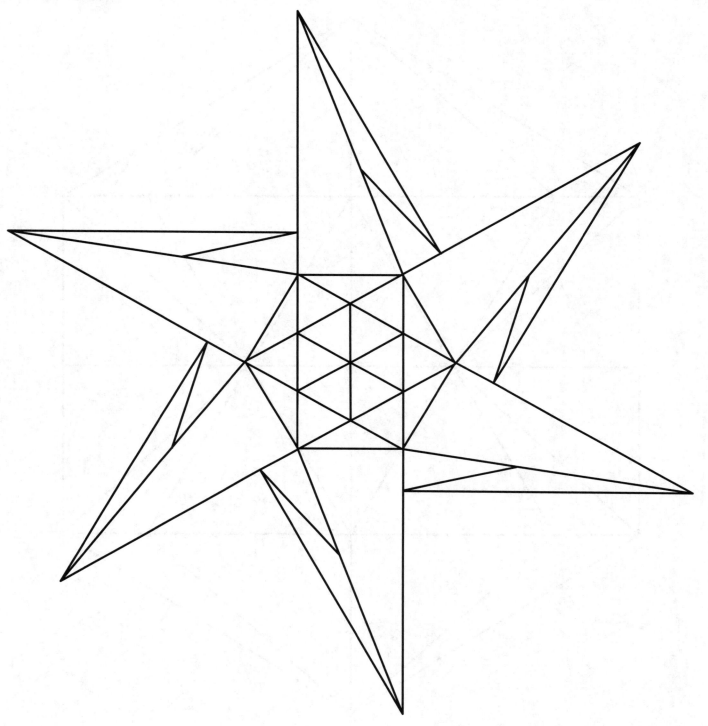

  **56**

Name: _____

Polly Want a Cracker?

Read the clues to identify each polygon.

> hexagon   octagon   pentagon   rectangle
> rhombus   square   trapezoid   triangle

1. I am a quadrilateral. Two of my sides are parallel, but two are not. What am I?

   _____

2. I am a polygon. I have eight sides and eight angles. Paint me red, and people will stop. What am I?

   _____

3. I am a parallelogram. My opposite sides are of equal length, but all four sides are not of equal length. What am I?

   _____

4. I am a parallelogram. All of my angles are right angles. My sides are always of equal length. What am I?

   _____

5. I am a polygon. I have six sides and six angles. What am I?

   _____

6. I am a polygon. I have three sides and three angles. What am I?

   _____

7. I am a polygon. I have five sides and five angles. What am I?

   _____

8. I am a parallelogram. My opposite angles are equal, but they do not have to be right angles. What am I?

   _____

Another Dimension

Identify each three-dimensional figure. Then, read the clues to identify each three-dimensional figure.

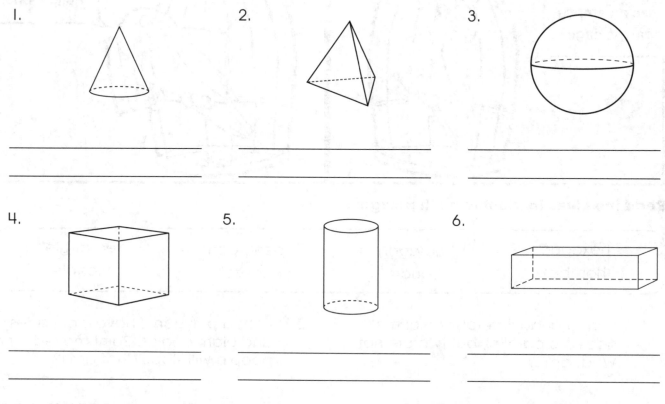

1. _____
   _____

2. _____
   _____

3. _____
   _____

4. _____
   _____

5. _____
   _____

6. _____
   _____

7. I am a three-dimensional figure. All of my faces are triangles. What am I?

   _____

8. I am a three-dimensional figure. I have a circular base and a vertex at my top. What am I?

   _____

9. I am a three-dimensional figure. My faces are parallel and congruent rectangles. What am I?

   _____

10. I am a three-dimensional figure. I have parallel circles at both ends and a curved surface. What am I?

    _____

11. I am a three-dimensional figure. All of my faces are square. What am I?

    _____

12. I am a three-dimensional figure. All of my points are at an equal distance from the center. What am I?

    _____

The Joke Is on You

Why can't you play jokes on snakes?

Because you can never "pull their legs."

Identify each set of figures as similar or congruent.

1. _____

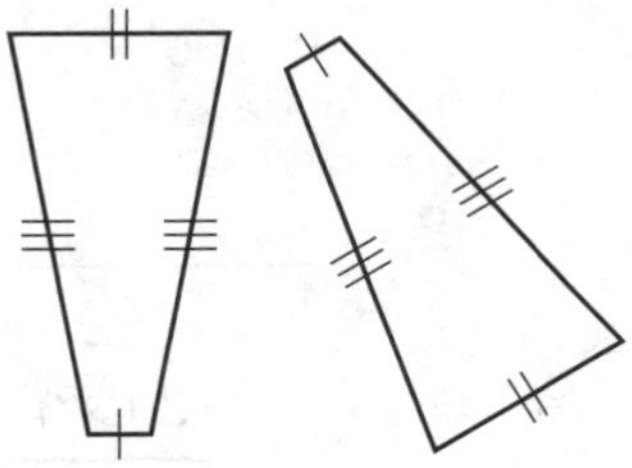

2. _____

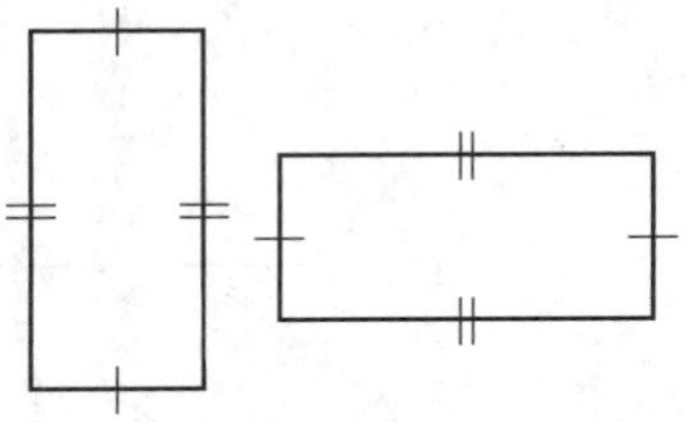

3. _____

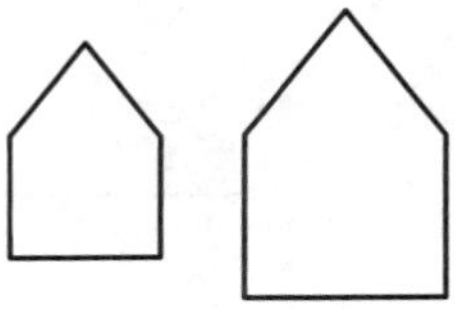

4. _____

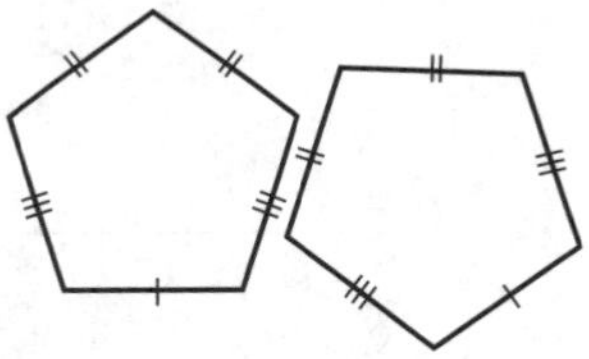

5. _____

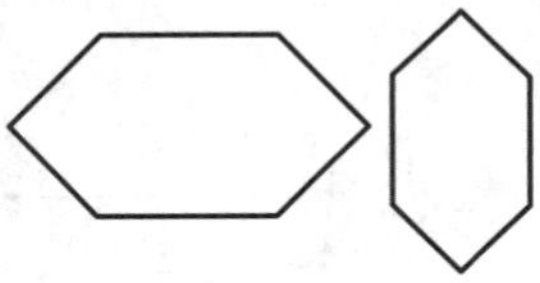

6. _____

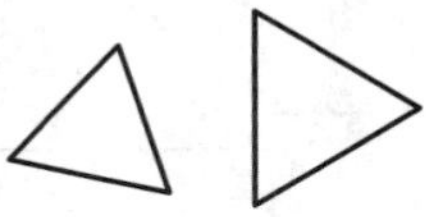

7. _____

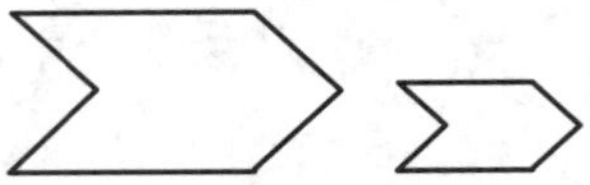

8. _____

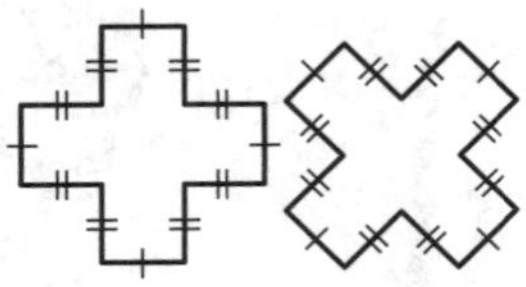

9. _____

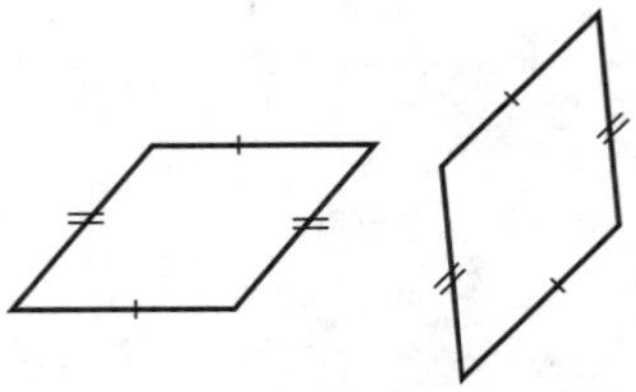

Measuring Up

Find the perimeter of each figure.

1.

15 mm

15 mm

P = _____

2.

2 cm

1 cm

P = _____

3.

3 ft.

1 ft.

P = _____

4.

6 mm   6 mm

4 mm

P = _____

5.

9 mm   9 mm

9 mm

P = _____

6.

6 in.

P = _____

7.

4 ft.

P = _____

8.

7 m

5 m

1 m

4 m

P = _____

9.

3 cm

5 cm   5 cm

6 cm

P = _____

10.

3 in.

5 in.   7 in.

6 in.

P = _____

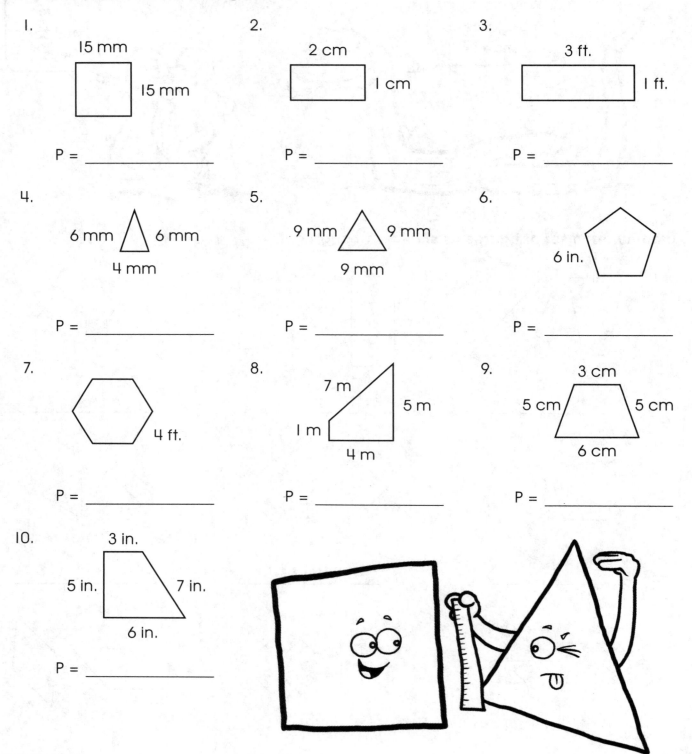

Name: _____

Well Hidden

Find the area of each figure. Match each answer with the correct letter in the key. To solve the riddle, write the letters in order on the answer lines.

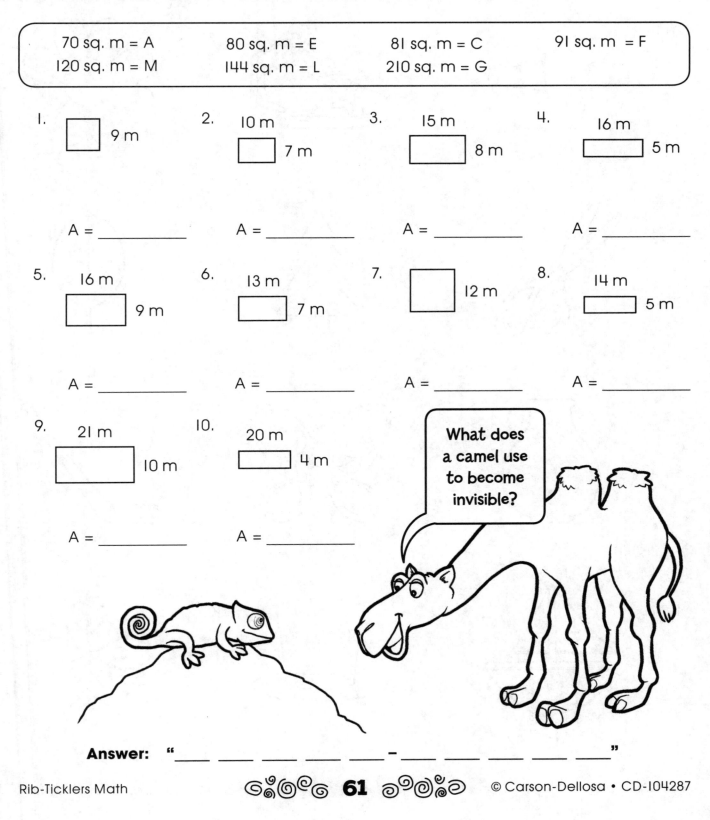

70 sq. m = A	80 sq. m = E	81 sq. m = C	91 sq. m = F
120 sq. m = M	144 sq. m = L	210 sq. m = G	

1. 9 m

A = _____

2. 10 m / 7 m

A = _____

3. 15 m / 8 m

A = _____

4. 16 m / 5 m

A = _____

5. 16 m / 9 m

A = _____

6. 13 m / 7 m

A = _____

7. 12 m

A = _____

8. 14 m / 5 m

A = _____

9. 21 m / 10 m

A = _____

10. 20 m / 4 m

A = _____

What does a camel use to become invisible?

Answer: "___ ___ ___ ___ ___ – ___ ___ ___ ___ ___"

Draw the Lines

Draw all of the lines of symmetry on each object. Cross out the object if it does not have a line of symmetry.

1.

2.

3.

4.

5.

6.

7.

8.

9.

10.

11.

12.

Stuffing

Find the coordinates of each point on the grid. To solve the riddle, match each set of coordinates to the coordinates below and write the letters on the answer lines.

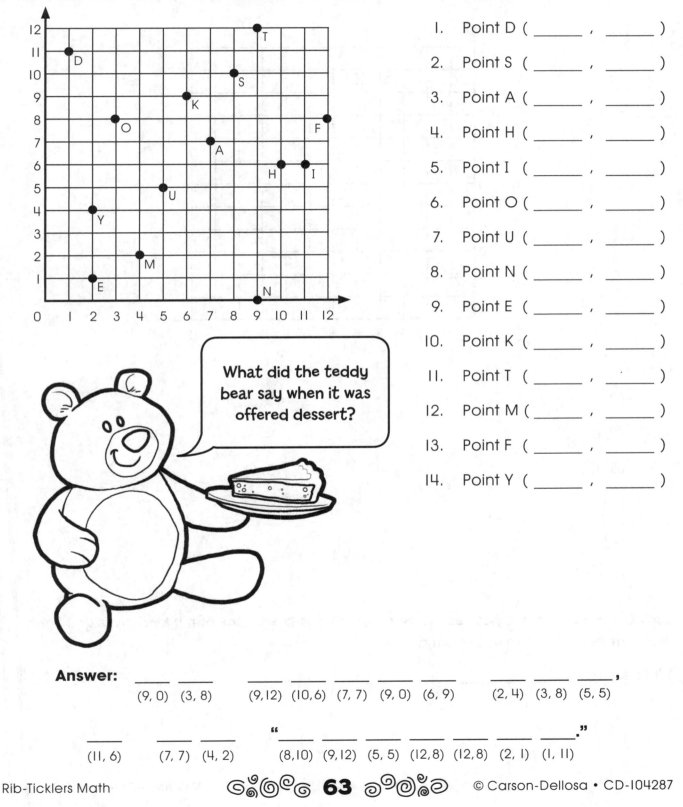

1. Point D (_____ , _____)

2. Point S (_____ , _____)

3. Point A (_____ , _____)

4. Point H (_____ , _____)

5. Point I (_____ , _____)

6. Point O (_____ , _____)

7. Point U (_____ , _____)

8. Point N (_____ , _____)

9. Point E (_____ , _____)

10. Point K (_____ , _____)

11. Point T (_____ , _____)

12. Point M (_____ , _____)

13. Point F (_____ , _____)

14. Point Y (_____ , _____)

What did the teddy bear say when it was offered dessert?

Answer: ____ ____ ____ ____ ____ ____ ____ ____ ____ ____ ,
(9, 0) (3, 8) (9,12) (10,6) (7, 7) (9, 0) (6, 9) (2, 4) (3, 8) (5, 5)

____ ____ ____ " ____ ____ ____ ____ ____ ____ ____."
(11, 6) (7, 7) (4, 2) (8,10) (9,12) (5, 5) (12,8) (12,8) (2, 1) (1, 11)

Shed Some Light

Use the coordinates below to plot each point on the grid. To solve the riddle, connect the points in order.

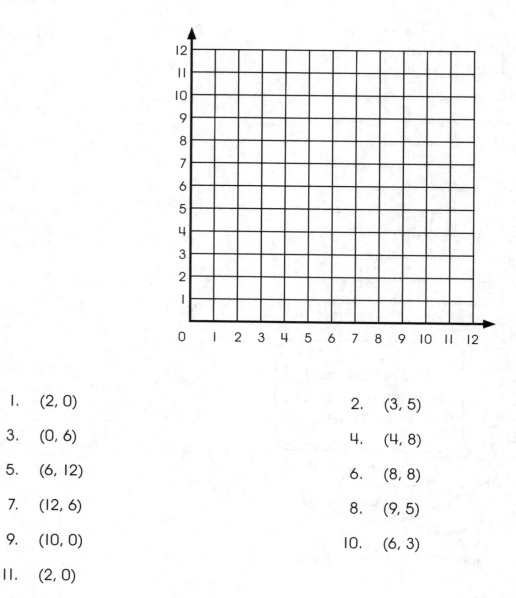

1. (2, 0)   2. (3, 5)

3. (0, 6)   4. (4, 8)

5. (6, 12)   6. (8, 8)

7. (12, 6)   8. (9, 5)

9. (10, 0)   10. (6, 3)

11. (2, 0)

Look up and you might not see me, but I am always there. One of my kind gives you light, while the rest of us live in the dark.

What am I? _____

Bright Ideas

Find the value of *n* in each problem. To solve the riddle, match the answers to the numbers below and write the correct letters on the answer lines. Hint: Some of the letters will be used more than once.

1. $4 \times n = 48$ **T**

   n =

2. $n - 39 = 37$ **O**

   n =

3. $n \div 7 = 5$ **M**

   n =

4. $13 + n = 21$ **I**

   n =

5. $n \div 4 = 5$ **S**

   n =

6. $n \times 8 = 72$ **H**

   n =

7. $n - 23 = 35$ **B**

   n =

8. $3 \times n = 30$ **U**

   n =

9. $19 + n = 67$ **N**

   n =

10. $67 - n = 37$ **R**

    n =

11. $n \times 7 = 77$ **C**

    n =

12. $n \div 7 = 4$ **A**

    n =

13. $n + 24 = 47$ **W**

    n =

14. $n - 8 = 34$ **G**

    n =

15. $n \div 5 = 3$ **E**

    n =

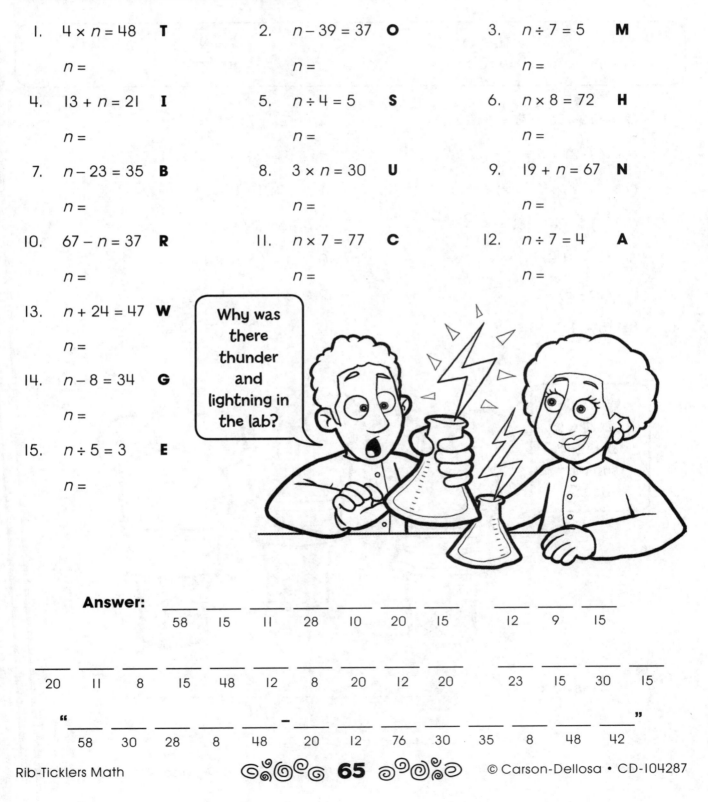

Why was there thunder and lightning in the lab?

Answer: __ __ __ __ __ __ __   __ __ __
58 15 11 28 10 20 15   12 9 15

__ __ __ __ __ __ __ __ __ __   __ __ __ __
20 11 8 15 48 12 8 20 12 20   23 15 30 15

" __ __ __ __   -   __ __ __ __ __ __ __ __ "
58 30 28 8   48 20 12 76 30 35 8 48 42

Frozen Treats

Use the order of operations to solve each problem. Match each answer with the correct letter in the key. To solve the riddle, write the letters in order on the answer lines.
Hint: The order of operations is parentheses, multiply or divide, then add or subtract.

2 = E	5 = O	7 = S	9 = N	12 = I
21 = A	23 = M	30 = C	34 = R	

1. $(7 + 8) + (56 \div 7) =$

2. $(21 \div 7) \times 4 =$

3. $6 + (6 - 2) \times 6 =$

4. $(4 + 6) \div (9 - 4) =$

5. $(7 \times 3 + 3) + (4 + 2) =$

6. $7 \times 4 + 8 - 2 =$

7. $(3 \times 4) \div (24 - 18) =$

8. $16 + 10 \div 2 =$

9. $60 \div 5 + 11 =$

10. $3 + 6 \times 4 + 3 =$

11. $4 \times (10 - 8) - 3 =$

12. $34 - 5 \times (11 - 6) =$

13. $8 - (5 + 43) \div 8 =$

14. $(16 - 2) \div (7 - 5) =$

What do cats like to eat on hot summer days?

Answer: "____ ____ ____ ____"   ____ ____ ____ ____

____ ____ ____ ____

Name: _____

You Be the Judge

Use the order of operations to solve each problem. Match each answer with the correct letter in the key. To solve the riddle, write the letters in order on the answer lines.
Hint: The order of operations is parentheses, multiply or divide, then add or subtract.

1 = U	3 = C	4 = T	5 = H	6 = E
7 = O	9 = N	11 = I	13 = R	15 = D

1. $(29 - 8) \div (7 - 4) =$

2. $(12 \div 2) + (3 \times 3) =$

3. $(5 \times 3 - 1) \div (7 - 5) =$

4. $9 + (8 - 2 \times 2) =$

5. $3 + 2 \times 4 =$

6. $(41 - 5) \div (7 - 3) =$

7. $(2 \times 7) - (2 \times 5) =$

8. $14 - (4 + 3) - 2 =$

9. $90 - (3 + 9) \times 7 =$

10. $7 - (30 - 2) \div 7 =$

11. $4 + 27 \div (4 + 5) =$

12. $(16 - 7) - (2 \times 4) =$

13. $4 + (10 - 7) \times 3 =$

14. $(35 - 7) \div (9 - 2) =$

What did the judge say when a skunk walked into the courtroom?

Judge

Answer: "___ ___ ___ ___" ___ ___   ___ ___ ___

___ ___ ___ ___!

Name: _____ properties

Clear as Day

Use the information below to identify the property of each equation.

> **Identity Property of Addition:** $a + 0 = a$
> **Identity Property of Multiplication:** $a \times 1 = a$
> **Associative Property of Addition:** $a + (b + c) = (a + b) + c$
> **Associative Property of Multiplication:** $a \times (b \times c) = (a \times b) \times c$
> **Commutative Property of Addition:** $a + b = b + a$
> **Commutative Property of Multiplication:** $a \times b = b \times a$
> **Distributive Property:** $a \times (b + c) = (a \times b) + (a \times c)$

1. $(2 + 5) + 4 = 2 + (5 + 4)$

    _____

2. $8 \times 10 = 10 \times 8$

    _____

3. $7 + 2 = 2 + 7$

    _____

4. $2 \times (4 + 5) = (2 \times 4) + (2 \times 5)$

    _____

5. $5 \times (3 \times 2) = (5 \times 3) \times 2$

    _____

6. $9 \times 1 = 9$

    _____

7. $(9 + 3) + 4 = 9 + (3 + 4)$

    _____

8. $7 + 0 = 7$

    _____

9. $3 + 6 = 6 + 3$

    _____

10. $(6 + 7) \times 3 = (6 \times 3) + (7 \times 3)$

    _____

11. $(4 \times 2) \times 5 = 4 \times (2 \times 5)$

    _____

12. $3 \times 2 = 2 \times 3$

    _____

Batter Up

Find the mean of each set of numbers. Match each answer with the correct letter in the key. To solve the riddle, write the letters in order on the answer lines.

4 = T	5 = I	6 = A	7 = G	8 = S
9 = O	10 = D	11 = E	12 = B	13 = R

1. 7, 4, 4

   Mean = _____

2. 8, 2, 2

   Mean = _____

3. 6, 6, 3, 5

   Mean = _____

4. 9, 7, 8

   Mean = _____

5. 5, 5, 9, 5

   Mean = _____

6. 7, 8, 4, 9

   Mean = _____

7. 6, 10, 11

   Mean = _____

8. 10, 8, 6, 12

   Mean = _____

9. 12, 9, 10, 9

   Mean = _____

10. 7, 10, 14, 17

   Mean = _____

11. 5, 4, 9, 6, 6

   Mean = _____

12. 3, 3, 4, 7, 3

   Mean = _____

13. 4, 2, 7, 6, 1

   Mean = _____

14. 14, 11, 11, 8

   Mean = _____

15. 10, 12, 17, 13

   Mean = _____

Why did the cake like to play baseball?

Answer: Because ____ ____ ____ ____ ____

____ ____ ____ ____ " ____ ____ ____ ____ ____ "

Practical Joker

What practical jokes do math teachers play?

"Arithme-tricks."

Find the median and the mode of each set of numbers.

1. 4, 6, 2, 7, 7

   Median = _____

   Mode = _____

2. 5, 9, 4, 2, 2

   Median = _____

   Mode = _____

3. 6, 11, 19, 6, 13

   Median = _____

   Mode = _____

4. 9, 7, 7, 17, 15

   Median = _____

   Mode = _____

5. 11, 10, 19, 11, 18

   Median = _____

   Mode = _____

6. 9, 14, 10, 9, 18

   Median = _____

   Mode = _____

7. 12, 18, 9, 8, 8

   Median = _____

   Mode = _____

8. 5, 8, 22, 5, 15

   Median = _____

   Mode = _____

9. 9, 13, 15, 8, 15

   Median = _____

   Mode = _____

10. 10, 10, 13, 12, 11

    Median = _____

    Mode = _____

11. 12, 17, 10, 9, 12

    Median = _____

    Mode = _____

12. 10, 13, 8, 9, 13

    Median = _____

    Mode = _____

On the 'Net

Use the table to answer each question.

Popular Joke Web Sites

Web Site	Visitors
R U Hilarious?	83,121
"Laps" in Comedy	58,452
Web of Puns	70,907
Quiet Quippers	46,162
Drop Me a Punch Line	49,323

1. Which Web site was the least popular? _____

2. Which Web site was the most popular? _____

3. How many more visitors did the most popular site receive than the least popular site? _____

4. How many more visitors did Web of Puns receive than "Laps" in Comedy?

_____

5. How many fewer visitors did Drop Me a Punch Line receive than "Laps" in Comedy? _____

6. What is the average number of people who visited these Web sites? Hint: Divide the total number of visitors by the number of Web sites. _____

Cold Comforts

Use the line graph to answer each question.

Monthly Snowfall in Mountaintop, Colorado

1. Between which two months was the greatest decrease in snowfall?

   _____

2. Between which two months was the greatest increase in snowfall?

   _____

3. How much more snow fell in March than in June? _____

4. How much more snow fell in November than in September? _____

5. How much total snow fell during the year? _____

72

Famous Places

Where do famous people shop?

At the "Mall of Fame."

Use the bar graph to answer each question.

Money Spent at the Mall

Amount Spent

$100.00
$90.00
$80.00
$70.00
$60.00
$50.00
$40.00
$30.00
$20.00
$10.00

Cody   Audrey   Lonny   Ava   Quan   Isabella   Melvin   Olivia

Shoppers

1. Who spent the most money at the mall? _____

2. Who spent the least money at the mall? _____

3. How much more money did Melvin spend than Cody? _____

4. How much less money did Audrey spend than Olivia? _____

5. Which shoppers spent the same amount of money? _____

6. What was the mean, or average, amount of money spent at the mall?
   Hint: Divide the total amount spent by the number of shoppers. _____

Page 4

1. >; 2. >; 3. <; 4. >; 5. =; 6. <; 7. <; 8. >; 9. <; 10. =;
11. <; 12. =; 13. >; 14. <; 15. =; 16. >; 17. >; 18. <;
19. >; 20. >; Because she wanted to "test" the waters

Page 5

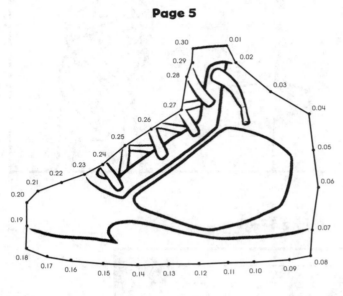

A shoe

Page 6

Answers are listed with the estimated sum first
and the original sum second. 1. 7,000; 7,308;
2. 4,000; 3,936; 3. 8,000; 7,591; 4. 5,000; 4,941;
5. 9,000; 8,992; 6. 7,000; 7,356; 7. 8,000; 7,931;
8. 6,000; 6,393; 9. 10,000; 9,571; 10. 7,000; 7,489;
11. 9,000; 8,710; 12. 10,000; 9,631

Page 7

1. 51,263; 2. 16,311; 3. 38,525; 4. 66,418; 5. 87,478;
6. 713,923; 7. 639,121; 8. 827,677; 9. 827,677;
10. 713,923; 11. 75,317; 12. 75,317; 13. 41,984;
14. 95,175; 15. 26,127; A frog with hiccups

Page 8

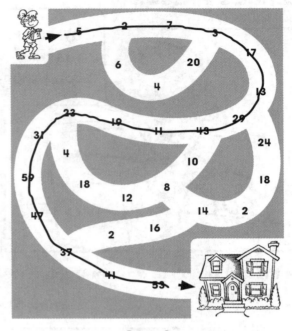

Page 9

1. 144; 2. 7,182; 3. 144; 4. 6,708; 5. 93; 6. 889;
7. 6,708; 8. 1,033; 9. 889; 10. 516; 11. 7,182;
12. 6,708; 13. 1,033; 14. 144; Because he had
"bat" breath

Page 10

1. 876; 2. 1,767; 3. 1,881; 4. 999; 5. 1,420; 6. 2,996;
7. 3,488; 8. 3,643; 9. 8,134; 10. 7,508; 11. 8,999;
12. 3,860; 13. 10,814; 14. 11,095; 15. 6,603;
16. 6,989; Because they like "trick" questions

Page 11

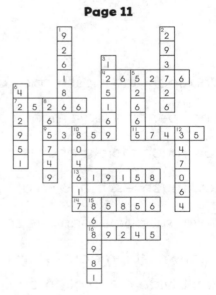

Page 12

1. 12.17; 2. 32.29; 3. 9.36; 4. 8.41; 5. 11.20; 6. 37.12; 7. 12.17; 8. 20.96; 9. 11.89; 10. 8.21; 11. 11.20; 12. 15.66; 13. 22.77; A decimal point

Page 13

1. 19; 2. 16; 3. 20; 4. 910; 5. 578; 6. 277; 7. 367; 8. 674; 9. 679; 10. 3,973; 11. 6,830; 12. 2,461; 13. 5,390; 14. 1,808; 15. 806; Because there are too many "cheetahs"

Page 14

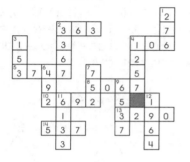

Page 15

Page 16

1. 3.77; 2. 42.24; 3. 8.11; 4. 10.71; 5. 63.51; 6. 2.01; 7. 17.24; 8. 22.91; 9. 73.21; 10. 13.66; 11. 3.25; 12. 0.16; 13. 2.60; 14. 32.38; 15. 1.31; 16. 1.29; It has to do a lot of "ketchup."

Page 17

1. 14,877 people; 2. 3,654 empty seats; 3. 112.8 miles; 4. $13.89 more; 5. 259,063 people; 6. 72,526 more people

Page 18

1. 210; 2. 320; 3. 90; 4. 420; 5. 80; 6. 360; 7. 120; 8. 560; 9. 300; 10. 240; 11. 540; 12. 480; 13. 350; 14. 150; 15. 180; 16. 100; Because it only knows how to "play"

Page 19

1. 410; 2. 388; 3. 246; 4. 266; 5. 528; 6. 603; 7. 162; 8. 306; 9. 476; 10. 295; 11. 72; 12. 164; Let's "go out" one of these nights.

Page 20

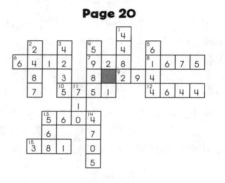

Page 21

1. 968; 2. 989; 3. 900; 4. 408; 5. 651; 6. 143; 7. 880; 8. 765; 9. 861; 10. 693; 11. 770; 12. 495; 13. 930; 14. 396; 15. 224; When you are doing multiplication

Page 22

1. 486; 2. 825; 3. 2,400; 4. 6,305; 5. 1,520; 6. 3,003; 7. 1,105; 8. 1,520; 9. 1,296; 10. 3,604; 11. 1,520; 12. 825; 13. 2,400; 14. 999; 15. 2,400; 16. 2,112; I've got you "covered."

Page 23

Page 24

1. 60 apples; 2. 144 biscuits; 3. 640 pretzel rods;
4. 234 blueberries; 5. 425 pieces of fruit;
6. 768 crackers

Page 25

1. 7; 2. 6; 3. 10; 4. 9; 5. 4; 6. 5; 7. 8; 8. 3; 9. 5; 10. 7;
11. 7; 12. 6; 13. 10; 14. 1; 15. 5; 16. 8; 17. 2; 18. 12;
Because they forgot the words

Page 26

1. 5 r7; 2. 3 r6; 3. 7 r6; 4. 5 r4; 5. 7 r3; 6. 9 r8;
7. 7 r7; 8. 6 r5; 9. 2 r2; 10. 8 r3; 11. 9 r5; 12. 2 r1;
At the "barkery"

Page 27

1. 93; 2. 49; 3. 92; 4. 217; 5. 57; 6. 301; 7. 468;
8. 588; 9. 635; 10. 918; On lily "pads"

Page 28

1. 35 r6; 2. 92 r2; 3. 44 r4; 4. 43 r7; 5. 34 r6;
6. 25 r5; 7. 13 r8; 8. 58 r1; 9. 32 r6; 10. 59 r5;
A "solar" bear

Page 29

1. 43; 2. 24; 3. 43; 4. 55; 5. 82; 6. 19; 7. 43; 8. 37;
9. 55; 10. 19; A "bald" eagle

Page 30

1. 3 r2; 2. 4 r9; 3. 5 r6; 4. 9 r7; 5. 6 r3; 6. 8 r5; 7. 4 r8;
8. 2 r3; 9. 9 r5; 10. 7 r4; 11. 6 r9; 12. 8 r8;
He "dino-snores."

Page 31

1. 3 tickets; 2. 12 DVDs; 3. 6 movies; 4. 15 people;
5. 22 people; 6. 36 tickets

Page 32

Circled letters in Row 1: Y, O, U, M; Circled letters
in Row 2: I, S, S, O; Circled letters in Row 3: N,
E, H, U; Circled letters in Row 4: N, D, R, E, D;
Circled letters in Row 5: P, E, R; Circled letters in
Row 6: C, E, N, T; Circled letters in Row 7: O, F,
T; Circled letters in Row 8: H, E, S, H, O; Circled
letters in Row 9: T, S; Circled letters in Row 10: Y,
O, U; Circled letters in Row 11: D, O, N; Circled
letters in Row 12: O, T, T, A; Circled letters in
Row 13: K, E; "You miss one hundred percent of
the shots you do not take."

Page 33

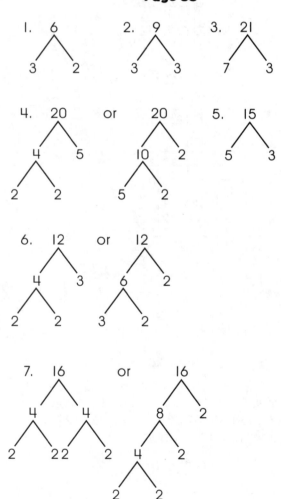

Answer Key

Page 33 (continued)

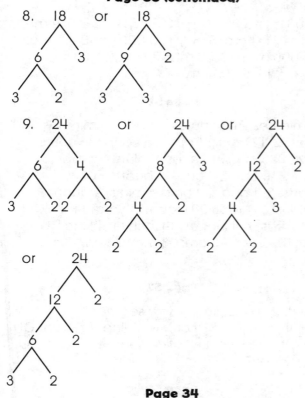

8. 18   or   18

9. 24   or   24   or   24

or   24

Page 34

1. 25; 2. 28; 3. 20; 4. 16; 5. 12; 6. 9; 7. 8; 8. 15;
9. 30; 10. 27; 11. 30; 12. 18; 13. 28; 14. 24;
Because it had more "cents"

Page 35

1. 9; 2. 11; 3. 2; 4. 7; 5. 4; 6. 3; 7. 5; 8. 12; 9. 15;
10. 6; 11. 12; 12. 4; I'm "stuck" on you.

Page 36

1. $\frac{2}{10}$; 2. $\frac{2}{4}$; 3. $\frac{9}{27}$; 4. $\frac{3}{18}$; 5. $\frac{8}{10}$; 6. $\frac{3}{9}$; 7. $\frac{4}{20}$;
8. $\frac{15}{25}$; 9. $\frac{2}{9}$; 10. $\frac{1}{4}$; 11. $\frac{1}{5}$; 12. $\frac{9}{18}$; 13. $\frac{3}{9}$;
14. $\frac{1}{5}$; 15. $\frac{2}{5}$; 16. $\frac{4}{5}$; 17. $\frac{3}{5}$; 18. $\frac{4}{6}$

Page 37

1. $\frac{1}{3}$; 2. $\frac{2}{7}$; 3. $\frac{1}{10}$; 4. $\frac{1}{4}$; 5. $\frac{5}{6}$; 6. $\frac{3}{5}$; 7. $\frac{2}{7}$;
8. $\frac{4}{5}$; 9. $\frac{1}{5}$; 10. $\frac{1}{10}$; 11. $\frac{1}{3}$; 12. $\frac{2}{5}$; 13. $\frac{2}{3}$;
14. $\frac{1}{5}$; 15. $\frac{1}{2}$; 16. $\frac{2}{5}$; 17. $\frac{1}{10}$; 18. $\frac{1}{6}$; 19. $\frac{3}{4}$;
20. $\frac{1}{3}$; To improve its Web "sight"

Page 38

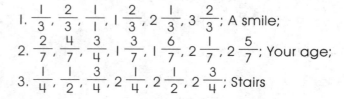

1. $\frac{39}{8}$; 2. $\frac{3}{2}$; 3. $\frac{17}{8}$; 4. $\frac{11}{3}$; 5. $\frac{39}{7}$; 6. $\frac{7}{2}$;
A towel; 7. $\frac{10}{3}$; 8. $\frac{23}{9}$; 9. $\frac{15}{4}$; 10. $\frac{19}{4}$; 11. $\frac{23}{5}$;
12. $\frac{17}{7}$; 13. $\frac{4}{3}$; A teapot

Page 39

1. $\frac{1}{3}$, $\frac{2}{3}$, $\frac{1}{1}$, 1$\frac{2}{3}$, 2$\frac{1}{3}$, 3$\frac{2}{3}$; A smile;
2. $\frac{2}{7}$, $\frac{4}{7}$, $\frac{3}{4}$, 1$\frac{3}{7}$, 1$\frac{6}{7}$, 2$\frac{1}{7}$, 2$\frac{5}{7}$; Your age;
3. $\frac{1}{4}$, $\frac{1}{2}$, $\frac{3}{4}$, 2$\frac{1}{4}$, 2$\frac{1}{2}$, 2$\frac{3}{4}$; Stairs

Page 40

1. $\frac{7}{8}$; 2. $\frac{5}{6}$; 3. $\frac{4}{5}$; 4. $\frac{3}{10}$; 5. $\frac{4}{7}$; 6. $\frac{9}{10}$;
7. $\frac{4}{7}$; 8. $\frac{3}{5}$; 9. $\frac{11}{12}$; 10. $\frac{2}{3}$; 11. $\frac{6}{7}$; 12. $\frac{6}{7}$;

When it is "full"

Page 41

1. $\frac{1}{3}$; 2. $\frac{2}{5}$; 3. $\frac{1}{4}$; 4. $\frac{1}{3}$; 5. $\frac{1}{2}$; 6. $\frac{1}{4}$; 7. $\frac{1}{7}$;
8. $\frac{2}{3}$; 9. $\frac{3}{5}$; 10. $\frac{5}{6}$; 11. $\frac{1}{5}$; 12. $\frac{1}{2}$; 13. $\frac{3}{5}$;
14. $\frac{1}{4}$; 15. $\frac{5}{6}$; A boa "constructor"

Page 42

1. $\frac{2}{15}$; 2. $\frac{2}{9}$; 3. $\frac{1}{3}$; 4. $\frac{1}{5}$; 5. $\frac{3}{7}$; 6. $\frac{4}{5}$; 7. $\frac{5}{12}$;
8. $\frac{3}{8}$; 9. $\frac{1}{6}$; 10. $\frac{1}{10}$; 11. $\frac{5}{7}$; 12. $\frac{2}{5}$; A "waist"

of paper

Page 43

1. $\frac{1}{6}$; 2. $\frac{1}{2}$; 3. $\frac{3}{5}$; 4. $\frac{1}{5}$; 5. $\frac{1}{4}$; 6. $\frac{3}{4}$; 7. $\frac{1}{2}$;
8. $\frac{1}{3}$; 9. $\frac{2}{3}$; 10. $\frac{5}{8}$; 11. $\frac{2}{5}$; 12. $\frac{4}{5}$; Ready,

set, "glow!"

Page 44

1. 0.8; 2. 0.9; 3. 0.5; 4. 0.4; 5. 0.76; 6. 0.2; 7. 0.75;
8. 0.05; 9. 0.3; 10. 0.68; 11. 0.25; 12. 0.02;
13. 0.1; 14. 0.6; 15. 0.56; Because she wanted a
"higher" education

Page 45

1. $\frac{8}{25}$; 2. $\frac{11}{100}$; 3. $\frac{11}{50}$; 4. $\frac{12}{25}$; 5. $\frac{21}{25}$; 6. $\frac{1}{10}$; 7. $\frac{2}{25}$;
8. $\frac{9}{10}$; 9. $\frac{51}{100}$; 10. $\frac{7}{10}$; 11. $\frac{1}{4}$; 12. $\frac{4}{5}$;

Because it is "two" tired

Page 46

1. the pepperoni pizza; 2. the sausage pizza;

3. A. 1 whole pizza or $\frac{3}{3}$ of a pizza; B. 1 whole

pizza or $\frac{3}{3}$ of a pizza is left; 4. A. 1 $\frac{1}{2}$ pizzas;

B. $\frac{1}{2}$ of a pizza is left

Page 47

1. 24 inches; 2. 6 feet; 3. 72 inches; 4. 4 feet;
5. 5,280 yards; 6. 10,560 feet; 7. 63,360 inches;
8. 4 yards; 9. 144 inches; 10. 3 feet; 11. 4 miles;
12. 26,400 feet; 13. 3 yards; 14. 15 feet;
15. 36 inches; 16. 3 miles; 17. 10 feet; 18. 2 miles;
19. 180 inches; 20. 60 inches

Page 48

1. 4 cups; 2. 15 pints; 3. 7 quarts; 4. 2 gallons;
5. 3 cups; 6. 5 pints; 7. 12 cups; 8. 4 gallons;
9. 5 gallons; 10. 14 cups; 11. 8 quarts;
12. 16 quarts; A "flour" garden

Page 49

1. 10 pounds; 2. 80 ounces; 3. 160,000 ounces;
4. 144 ounces; 5. 2 tons; 6. 14,000 pounds;
7. 4 tons; 8. 176 ounces; 9. 6,000 pounds;
10. 320,000 ounces; 11. 2 pounds; 12. 48 ounces;
13. 6 pounds; 14. 112 ounces; 15. 8 pounds;
16. 6 tons; 17. 12 pounds; 18. 640 ounces;
19. 32,000 ounces; 20. 2 tons

Page 50

1. 2,000 mL; 2. 25,000 g; 3. 19 L; 4. 32 L; 5. 4 m;
6. 19 km; 7. 11 cm; 8. 8 g; 9. 6,000 m; 10. 40 mg;
11. 36,000 mm; 12. 70 mL; 13. 4 kL; 14. 5 m;
15. 41 cg; 16. 5,200 cm

Page 51

1. 15 minutes, 30 minutes, 1 hour, 70 minutes,
2 hours; 2. 12 hours, 1 day, 25 hours, 36 hours,
2 days; 3. 5 cups, 15 cups, 9 pints, 1 gallon,
5 quarts; 4. 1 pint, 3 cups, 1 quart, 3 pints,
2 quarts; 5. 1 quart, 4 pints, 6 pints, 4 quarts,
3 gallons; 6. 1 foot, 30 inches, 1 yard, 1 mile,
1,800 yards; 7. 4 inches, 14 inches, 44 inches,
4 feet, 4 yards; 8. 3 cm, 33 mm, 33 cm, 3 m,
3 km

Page 52

1. point; 2. ray; 3. line; 4. line segment;
5. point Q; 6. line MN or $\overleftrightarrow{MN}$; 7. line segment CD
or $\overline{CD}$; 8. line EF or $\overleftrightarrow{EF}$; 9. line segment PQ or $\overline{PQ}$;
10. ray ZY or $\overrightarrow{ZY}$

Page 53

1. parallel, R; 2. parallel, E; 3. perpendicular, C;
4. perpendicular, E; 5. intersecting, S;
6. intersecting, S; 7. parallel, P; 8. perpendicular,
I; 9. parallel, E; 10. intersecting, C;
11. perpendicular, E; 12. intersecting, S;
"Recess" pieces

Page 54

1. right; 2. obtuse; 3. acute; 4. acute; 5. obtuse;
6. acute; 7. right; 8. obtuse; 9. right

Answer Key

Page 55

Color key: green (right triangle) = 1
blue (obtuse triangle) = 2
purple (acute triangle) = 3

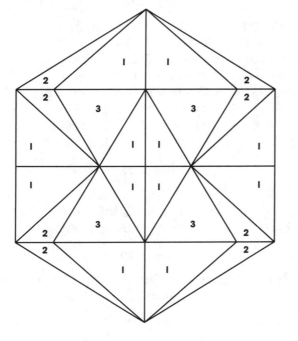

Page 56

Color key: orange (isosceles triangle) = 1
red (equilateral triangle) = 2
yellow (scalene triangle) = 3

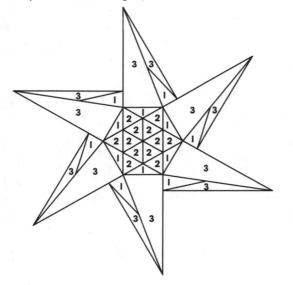

Page 57

1. trapezoid; 2. octagon; 3. rectangle;
4. square; 5. hexagon; 6. triangle; 7. pentagon;
8. rhombus

Page 58

1. cone; 2. triangular pyramid; 3. sphere;
4. cube; 5. cylinder; 6. rectangular prism;
7. triangular pyramid; 8. cone; 9. rectangular
prism; 10. cylinder; 11. cube; 12. sphere

Page 59

1. congruent; 2. congruent; 3. similar;
4. congruent; 5. similar; 6. similar; 7. similar;
8. congruent; 9. congruent

Page 60

1. 60 mm; 2. 6 cm; 3. 8 ft.; 4. 16 mm; 5. 27 mm;
6. 30 in.; 7. 24 ft.; 8. 17 m; 9. 19 cm; 10. 21 in.

Page 61

1. 81 sq. m; 2. 70 sq. m; 3. 120 sq. m; 4. 80 sq. m;
5. 144 sq. m; 6. 91 sq. m; 7. 144 sq. m; 8. 70 sq. m;
9. 210 sq. m; 10. 80 sq. m; "Camel-flage"

Page 62

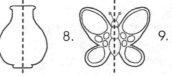

Answer Key

Page 63

1. (1, 11); 2. (8, 10); 3. (7, 7); 4. (10, 6); 5. (11, 6);
6. (3, 8); 7. (5, 5); 8. (9, 0); 9. (2, 1); 10. (6, 9);
11. (9, 12); 12. (4, 2); 13. (12, 8); 14. (2, 4);
No thank you, I am "stuffed."

Page 64

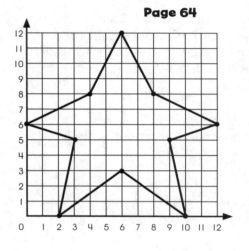

A star

Page 65

1. 12; 2. 76; 3. 35; 4. 8; 5. 20; 6. 9; 7. 58; 8. 10;
9. 48; 10. 30; 11. 11; 12. 28; 13. 23; 14. 42; 15. 15;
Because the scientists were "brain-storming"

Page 66

1. 23; 2. 12; 3. 30; 4. 2; 5. 30; 6. 34; 7. 2; 8. 21;
9. 23; 10. 30; 11. 5; 12. 9; 13. 2; 14. 7; "Mice"
cream cones

Page 67

1. 7; 2. 15; 3. 7; 4. 13; 5. 11; 6. 9; 7. 4; 8. 5; 9. 6;
10. 3; 11. 7; 12. 1; 13. 13; 14. 4; "Odor" in the court!

Page 68

1. Associative Property of Addition;
2. Commutative Property of Multiplication;
3. Commutative Property of Addition;
4. Distributive Property; 5. Associative Property
of Multiplication; 6. Identity Property of
Multiplication; 7. Associative Property of
Addition; 8. Identity Property of Addition;
9. Commutative Property of Addition;
10. Distributive Property; 11. Associative Property
of Multiplication; 12. Commutative Property of
Multiplication

Page 69

1. 5; 2. 4; 3. 5; 4. 8; 5. 6; 6. 7; 7. 9; 8. 9; 9. 10;
10. 12; 11. 6; 12. 4; 13. 4; 14. 11; 15. 13; Because it
is a good "batter"

Page 70

1. Median = 6; Mode = 7; 2. Median = 4;
Mode = 2; 3. Median = 11; Mode = 6;
4. Median = 9; Mode = 7; 5. Median = 11;
Mode = 11; 6. Median = 10; Mode = 9;
7. Median = 9; Mode = 8; 8. Median = 8;
Mode = 5; 9. Median = 13; Mode = 15;
10. Median = 11; Mode = 10; 11. Median = 12;
Mode = 12; 12. Median = 10; Mode = 13

Page 71

1. Quiet Quippers; 2. R U Hilarious?;
3. 36,959 more visitors; 4. 12,455 more visitors;
5. 9,129 fewer visitors; 6. 61,593 people

Page 72

1. March and April; 2. October and November;
3. 7 inches; 4. 9 inches; 5. 105 inches

Page 73

1. Olivia; 2. Isabella; 3. $25.00 more;
4. $30.00 less; 5. Lonny and Ava; 6. $72.50